Index of Content

Preface..3
Introduction..5
PART 1. CONSCIOUSNESS..........................6
Three Secrets of the Universe.....................................6
Wave Function..12
Fundamental Blocks of Mentality 15
Matter..18
Relationship between Matter and Consciousness 20
Laws...23
Life..25
Cognition..27
Memory and Perception...29
Personality and Egregores 31
PART 2. CONTACT WITH PLATO'S WORLD.............34
Why Are We Alone in the Universe?..........................34
Planetary Consciousness 38
Evolution..41
Waves Vs. Ego (Elementals) 46
Broken Mirror...50
The Universe as a Thought of the Demiurge 53
The Universe that Does Not Exist............................56
PART 3. REALITY 60
Holographic Principle...60
Space...64
Spiritual Reality 68
Physical Reality 72
Wave Function Collapse...78
Information Paradox..82
Consciousness vs. Black Holes.................................86
PART 4. WHERE DOES TIME END?......................89
Time 89
Clairvoyance and Déjà Vu......................................91
Platonic Ideas...94
The Universe Green Door 98

Epilogue 104
Bibliography..106

Preface

The universe within which we exist - from where and why did all this come about? Whose hand or will created it, by whose written or unwritten laws it is evolving? For what purpose do we exist in this world? What further fate awaits it? Probably, each person thought about these questions at least once in his life.

During the course of our lives, the acuteness of these issues, against the backdrop of everyday routine, either weakens, or we get content with intermediate, incomplete pictures of the universe. In particular, most of us, at a certain stage in life, take the side of a scientific, or a religious view of the world.

The scientific worldview is based upon (although it is not a universal rule) a belief in Charles Darwin's theory of evolution, and, in many cases, atheism. Religious worldview, in turn, often stops at faith in the creation of our world by God - while avoiding further consideration of all the circumstances of the creation of the universe, in particular, the apparent imperfection of the material world. For example, Gautama Buddha is credited with saying that questions about the origin of our world are idle. Christianity also, in its turn, contains almost no information about the circumstances of our world creation.

Further progress in understanding the universe is impossible without the synthesis of scientific and religious approaches. Scientific knowledge can be supplemented and enriched by an open recognition of the fundamental role of consciousness in the universe. Religion, in turn, by its nature does not necessarily intersect with scientific knowledge, but the expanded perspective, supplemented by science, on our world is an undoubted plus for mystically thinking people. Ultimately, the Truth about our world is common to all of us.

This book was the result of many years of reflection and discussion on the problems of the universe, taking into account the religious, scientific and philosophical experience of many other authors. At the same time, my goal was not to retell an already existing, well-known material - whether from science or religion. The main content of this book is primarily in the presentation of new ideas and hypotheses. Acquaintance with the popular science literature on physics will help the reader in understanding the material of chapters devoted to scientific topics. Similarly, a religious, mystical mindset will facilitate the perception of those chapters where the book goes into mystical questions.

The author hopes that the original hypotheses presented in this book about the nature of space and time, the driving force of evolution, the role of consciousness and platonic ideas in the formation of the world, will open up a new perspective for the reader to the key questions of the universe.

Introduction

Modern science faces a number of fundamental questions, such as the origin of the universe, the mystery of evolution, the enigmatic laws of quantum mechanics, the nature of consciousness, space, and time. On the other hand, similar questions of creation – the origin of the world, the role of man in it, the nature of good and evil – have been the subject matter of concern for many world religions and various kinds of mystical teachings for ages.

Interaction and mutual understanding between these two fields of knowledge leave much to be desired. Traditionally, physicists do not embrace mysticism readily. The field of interest of scientists is delineated by the boundaries of the so-called "rigorous science". However, the objective course of events leads to the fact that, as it develops, science inevitably enters the mystical realm. The theory of evolution is a clear example of a boundary zone in which both these spheres of knowledge overlap. Another instance of a border region involves the question pertaining to the nature of consciousness.

Despite the circumspect attitude of science towards the issues of mysticism – it is difficult to overestimate the explanatory power of science. Modern physical theories are a treasure trove of information, which can be used to shed light on mystical questions as well. It can be said that, at present, a golden vein exists between mysticism and physics. The purpose of this book is to examine the key issues of the universe in an all-encompassing view – from a "scientific-mystical" perspective. This is possible because modern science has come in close proximity to the spiritual boundaries of the world. Also, there is an opposite connection in this regard – adequate philosophical intuitions can lead to promising directions when it comes to physical theory.

PART 1. CONSCIOUSNESS

Three Secrets of the Universe

There are three riddles associated with the peculiar meaningfulness of the universe.

1. Structured Nature of the Universe

The parameters of our universe (the strength of electromagnetic and strong nuclear interactions, the gravitational constant, the cosmological constant, the mass of the proton, and a number of others) are tuned in the finest way possible, enabling the existence of galaxies, stars, planets, and living organisms. This unique setting of parameters is conventionally explained through the anthropic principle. According to this principle, there are many lifeless alternative universes whose physical parameters lead to desolate worlds, in which there is nothing but radiation. We, according to the anthropic principle, were lucky to be in one of the worlds conducive to life. But, our existence is not the outcome of Divine Providence. To put it simply, in the context of the infinite number of lifeless worlds, sooner or later, one of them should have been fortunate with the physical parameters that make life possible.

2. The Phenomenon of Evolution

Darwin's theory of evolution is another instance of science's appeal to extraordinary luck. According to this theory, the emergence of the most complex living forms is due to the will of chance – a result of random, successful mutations of the genetic code. However, a simple assertion of combinatorics put an end to Darwinism, namely, its statement about the allegedly creative role of random mutations. In most cases, mutations are either useless or lead to degradation: genetic defects, cancer, and so on. At the same time, the creation of new, useful functionality in the body requires the programming of kilobytes of genetic code, which is unattainable through blind sampling. It is stated that evolution accidentally stumbles upon "successful" chains of code, which, in principle, are present in large amounts, and some of them, sooner or later, end up being discovered. However, the entire problem in this regard is that the number of useless chains is immeasurably greater!

Let's consider an example of acquisition by living creatures of the ability of active flight. The active flight was evolutionarily preceded by passive flight – the so-called "gliding". The gliders, beings with the ability of passive flight, had to discover a genetic chain that would grant them the ability of active flight (in practice, the changes affect not one but a lot of genes; but, the mathematical complexity, and therefore the probability assessment, is not affected by this).

The difference between passive and active flight is immense. The latter requires appropriate changes in the skeleton and, most importantly, the brain. For an active, guided flight, the ability to coordinate the movement of the wings is required, which, in turn, requires a reconstruction of the nervous system. Moreover, in the process of evolution from passive to active flight, there are no beneficial intermediate steps! For gliders, the action of waving their limbs is of no use – this only worsens their gliding, and they will not be able to fly actively anyway.

Suppose that the genetic chain providing the ability to active flight consists of only 1000 nucleotides (this is more than a conservative estimate). Thus, the evolution has to find one of the sets of genetic chains, 1000 elements in length, which transform the skeletons and brains of the gliders to meet the requirements of active flight.

We make a very conservative assumption – only one nucleotide out of four, at each step of the chain construction, fails to provide the desired result. According to combinatorial laws, the probability of randomly finding a useful coding strand of nucleotides is inversely proportional to the exponential of the number of nucleotides in such a chain.

According to our assumptions, the probability that evolution will successfully find a useful code in one attempt is as follows:

$$P = (3/4)^{1000} = 0.1^{125}$$

On the other hand, the number of attempts (N) at the disposal of the evolution is expressed by a polynomial:

$$N = G * M * A$$

– where G represents the number of generations; M represents the number of population members in each generation; and A represents the number of attempts at creative mutations of the germ cell DNA.

Even if one chooses huge values for the parameters G, M, A, for example:

$G = 10^{12}$ (one trillion)

$M = 10^{15}$ (one quadrillion)

$A = 10^{18}$ (one quintillion)

The probability of finding one of the useful genetic chains in the entire set of generations will be as follows:

$$P * N = 0.1^{80}$$

– a vanishingly small value!

It is obvious that the exponential combinatorial law easily dominates the polynomial number of attempts that Darwinian evolution has.

The billions of years that were at the disposal of the evolutionary process are thoroughly inadequate for the random creation of DNA (or its analog – RNA), not to mention the constant addition of new and new functionality. Thus, "genetic variation" and "natural selection" are incapable of explaining either the emergence of life or the further evolution of forms.

3. The Phenomenon of Consciousness

The mysterious nature of consciousness manifests itself in our ability to conduct a meaningful conversation, the ability of mathematicians to find significant theorems in the boundless sea of trivial mathematical statements, and in many other forms of creativity. Computer programs, in spite of increasingly sophisticated techniques and advanced algorithms, are, in principle, incapable of solving problems that require insight. For instance, they are unable to pass the Turing test (maintaining a conversation), or even find the right move with respect to an elementary (for a human being) chess position:

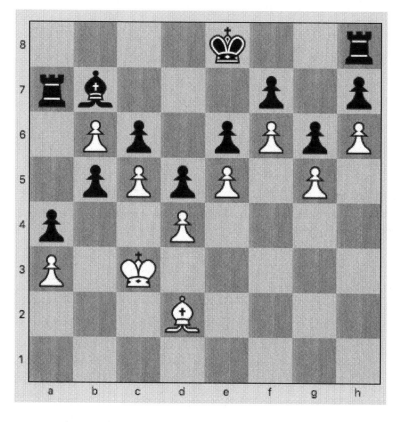

(White to move)

Conclusions

Considering all the three points in the aggregate, their similarity is striking. In all three cases – the unique selection of physical constants of the universe, the ability of the evolution to code new functionality, and the faculty of the human consciousness to procure insight – we observe the same repetitive property – finding unique, useful states in an endless ocean of "junk".

We can assume that the solution to any of the three aforementioned riddles contains the answer for the remaining two. Best of all, we are familiar with the third, that is, with our own consciousness. Extrapolating the ability of our consciousness to meaningful creativity – we can conclude that the emergence of the universe in all of its complexity, as well as the phenomenon of evolution, is also explained by the creative activity of the consciousness.

Just as we write meaningful text (rather than mumbo-jumbo), the evolution consciously finds useful genetic chains that are thousands-of-nucleotides long, and the universe discovers the unique laws of physics that make the existence of stars, planets, and life possible.

But, what is this consciousness about? Based on the Buddhist concept of *anātman*, this consciousness is one for all. The very consciousness, whose voice we perceive as our own, is responsible for the emergence of the universe, as well as for the creation and evolution of life.

This idea provides a concise explanation for the imperfection of the universe. Why is there mutual devouring among living organisms? Why is the universe so far from being the heaven that our imagination can conceive? To answer these questions, it is sufficient to look inside ourselves.

Wave Function

According to modern science, all material objects of our world, including all known types of physical interactions (weak and strong nuclear forces, electromagnetism, and gravitation) are subject to the laws of quantum mechanics – the key concept of which is the "wave function".

The *wave function* describes the state of a quantum system at a given time. The dynamics of the wave function is described by the linear Schrödinger equation. Evolving in accordance with the Schrödinger equation, the quantum system behaves like a wave, acquiring many possible states simultaneously.

One of the key mysteries of quantum mechanics is that the quantum system does not always adhere to the Schrödinger equation. The exception to the rule is the so-called "quantum state reduction", which occurs when a quantum particle is measured. As a result of the quantum collapse, the quantum system selects one state among the set of possible states (or a whole subset of states, depending on how "complete" the measurement is).

A popular illustration of the wave function collapse is a classical double-slit experiment:

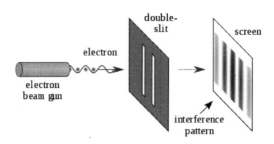

After the detector is positioned in the path of a quantum particle, the particle is forced to choose between two possible trajectories (slit A or slit B), as a result of which the wave function of the particle collapses, and the interference pattern on the screen disappears.

What is the underlying reason for the wave function collapse? How does the Schrödinger wave equation give way to a new process? In this regard, there are various theories, which include the following:

- According to Everett's *Many-Worlds theory*, no collapse actually occurs. Instead, at the moment of measurement of a quantum particle, the universe splits into two copies. In one copy, the quantum particle travels through slit A and through slit B in the other. Thus, the *many-worlds theory* denies the collapse of the quantum wave as such. According to this theory, a quantum particle realizes all of its possible states in alternative universes. The obvious problem with this theory is that Everett's multiverse means "runaway infinity" of ever-branching worlds.

- Another interpretation in this regard is the so-called "objective collapse". According to this model, the quantum system actually chooses one state from the set of possible ones. A quantum particle flies either through slit A or through slit B. In the model proposed by Roger Penrose, the collapse of the quantum system occurs when the curvature of its gravitational field reaches a critical level. The greater the mass of the quantum system, i.e., the stronger its gravitational field, the lesser curvature of the gravitational field is required for the onset of the collapse.

Irrespective of the interpretation of the quantum wave collapse, it is important to emphasize the fact that, whether apparent or real, the speed at which a quantum system collapses increases along with an increase in its size and an increase in the measure of disharmony between its constituent quantum particles.

Quantum collapse has a simple musical analogy. Imagine that quantum particles are musicians performing a symphony. This symphony is nothing but a wave function of the orchestra. While the musicians are playing harmoniously, the melody is developing according to the wave laws of quantum mechanics. However, if the musicians do not play in sync with one another, the symphony is replaced by cacophony, which is analogous to the collapse of the wave function. Certainly, the larger the number of musicians in the orchestra, the harder it is to coordinate their performance.

Fundamental Blocks of Mentality

What are primary constituents of physical reality? What is the difference between the material and the spiritual? Where is the distinguishing line between consciousness, living, and non-living matter?

The world comprises of fundamental blocks of existence – the length of which is of the order of the Planck length (if they have any size at all). It is logical to assume that the fundamental blocks of existence should be the root cause of all the phenomena in our world without exception, the most unique of which is the phenomenon of consciousness. For this reason, the fundamental blocks of existence can be called the "fundamental blocks of mentality".

The *fundamental blocks of mentality* – this is what can be called pure consciousness. They, as well as their harmonious associations, stand behind all manifestations of consciousness in our world. This consciousness is present in elementary particles, living cells, insects, animals, humans, and ascending further along the ladder of spiritual beings, ending with the universe as a whole.

Consciousness is a phenomenon of the material world and should be explained by one of the known types of physical interactions. Somehow, our thoughts, heading out on their way in the fundamental blocks of mentality, are able to influence the activity of neurons, the size of which exceeds the Planck length by 28 orders! (the question regarding the physical mechanism mediating our thought process is considered in the chapter "The Universe as a Thought of the Demiurge").

Being the fundamental blocks of the universe, the fundamental blocks of mentality are beyond the reach of the scientific method. It is impossible to look at a section of space that is less than the Planck size in principle. To do this, we would require a photon with the appropriate resolution. In this case, as is known, the energy of the photon is inversely proportional to the length of its wave. At extremely small distances probed, the photon energy reaches critical values at which it collapses into a black hole. It is impossible to acquire the measurement result from a black hole in principle. Thus, nature reliably obscures the spiritual world from the reach of the scientific method.

Hence, the universe is built from the fundamental blocks that stand behind the most complex and unique phenomenon in this universe – consciousness. At the same time, there is another perspective about our world – the perception of the universe as a collection of all sorts of platonic ideas. This is indicated by the physics of our world, described by ideal mathematical laws, as well as our own experience – we perceive the world as a set of numerous logical, ethical, aesthetic, sensory ideas and sensations. Both these perspectives do not contradict but complement each other. We postulate a relation of the identity between the following key concepts:

- The fundamental blocks of existence
- Pure consciousness (fundamental blocks of mentality)
- Platonic ideas

Matter

If we look at matter under a microscope, predominantly, there will be emptiness. For example, if we imagine the nucleus of an atom being the size of a coin, then the distance from this nucleus to the orbit of the nearest electron will be equal to one mile! But, perhaps, if not the atom itself, then at least its nucleus, or electrons, are tangible material particles, a sort of diminished analog of a billiard ball? Far from it, an attempt to discern something "material" inside the nucleus of an atom, or the electron, will prove futile. For example the electron, being a quantum particle, is "smeared" in space around the nucleus of the atom, it is present literally everywhere – representing a completely unusual object, which has no analogs in the everyday world around us.

In fact, matter is a quantum field that cannot be touched. The same properties – the lack of materiality, permeability, omnipresence – are traditionally attributed to the spirit. It turns out that, at a microscopic level, matter and spirit are very similar to each other. This similarity is not accidental: both spirit and matter consist of one and the same primary substance – the *fundamental blocks of mentality.*

The difference between matter and spirit is not in terms of the tangibility of the former by our senses, but in its predictable, algorithmic behavior. Not all material particles are tangible (i.e. neutrino), but all material particles behave algorithmically.

Previously, we noted that consciousness is based on the fundamental blocks of the mentality and their harmonious associations. But, where harmony is absent, where the fundamental blocks of mentality collapse into the chaotic conflict of micro-wills, matter manifests itself:

Matter is the form of existence of a selfish spirit, incapable of incorporating more perfect and harmonious forms.

Matter is the broken mirror from the "The Snow Queen" – an allegory, despite its gloom, that reflects the essence of things.

In itself, matter represents the conflicting fragments of consciousness. But, whose consciousness? It is important to note that it is not consciousness that exists inside the material universe, but the material universe exists inside consciousness. This consciousness belongs to the Creator of our universe.

How did the spiritual entity, the Creator of our world, break up into fragments - gross, egoistic matter? What caused the creation of the Universe, which is almost devoid of creativity, subject to the second law of thermodynamics, and heading towards inevitable heat death? Was the Big Bang an act of creation or, on the contrary, a catastrophe? These questions will be considered in the following discussion.

Relationship between Matter and Consciousness

Quantum mechanics contains the notion *of wave-particle duality*. In the above double-slit experiment, the attempt to measure an electron leads to the fact that the latter goes only through one of the slits - i.e., behaves like a particle. However, in the absence of measurement, the same electron goes through both slits at the same time, after which it interferes with itself, leaving an interference pattern on the screen that is characteristic of the waves.

The wave-particle duality allows us to make a specific connection between two philosophical concepts - *spirit* and *matter*. Namely, the corpuscular (particle) state can be associated with matter, whereas the wave state can be associated with the spirit.

But, strictly speaking, individual particles cannot possess "corpuscular properties". A single particle is always a wave. Corpuscularity arises from the collapse of this wave when interacting with another particle. Thus, corpuscularity is not a property of single particles but of their groups and is a measure of the lack of harmony in a group.

The absence of harmony is a consequence of selfishness. A selfish spirit loses its wave nature and appears in the form of material particles. Matter is nothing more than a selfish, algorithmized form of the spirit's existence:

SPIRIT x EGOISM = MATTER

SPIRIT x LOVE = CONSCIOUSNESS

Is it possible to change from the material to spiritual form? As the example of the evolution of conscious beings (like ourselves) shows, the answer to this question is positive. The transformation of matter into a spiritual state can be called "enlightenment" – this term reflects the positive ethical nature of this process. As it enlightens, matter becomes more and more like consciousness. The enlightened matter is more harmonious; its wave nature takes form inside it increasingly.

In turn, what needs to happen to consciousness so that it can transform into matter? This is achieved through a "defilement" – a process of reverse *enlightenment*. During *defilement*, the selfishness of consciousness increases. The increase in egoism leads to a conflict between the wills of the particles, which constitute the consciousnesses, and forms the resulting laws. As the role of the laws increases, consciousness is deprived of its freedom, creativity, and is transformed into matter.

The more egoistic the consciousness, the more algorithmic and the less creative it is. Algorithmization of consciousness indicates that it behaves in the same way at all times, which in turn means that it can be described by the laws of physics.

Thus, we have a wave scale of the "spiritual or material", on the edges of which lies the following:

- *Spirit* – a state of absolute harmony, when all the fundamental blocks of the mentality are part of one quantum super-wave

- *Agga* – the corpuscular form of the spirit's existence, characterized by a complete loss of wave properties

Thus, 100% wave nature is *Spirit* whereas 100% corpuscularity is *Agga*. Between these two extremes, there are states of mind or matter with varying degrees of enlightenment.

At its core, the world is spiritual. There is only consciousness, but with varying degree of selfishness. The selfish, algorithmized consciousness of the universe is perceived by a comparatively more perfect human consciousness as "matter". Matter, thus, is an appearance – an illusion.

From the above, it follows that the concept of "material" is relative. There are beings – the Demiurges – with a much higher level of consciousness than ours. From their point of view, we, humanity, represent the similarity of matter. At our level of consciousness, the algorithmic laws of biology, economics, or sociology operate, just like the laws of physics – at the level of matter.

To the extent that egoism is present in humanity, we are a biomass whose next day is indistinguishable from the previous one. To the extent that love exists in mankind, we take the form of a single universal human consciousness, whose creative abilities are immeasurably higher than that of individual human beings.

Laws

How does matter acquire its algorithmic nature? What makes it obey the laws of physics?

If we place a hand on the wall, we will feel the reciprocal force. This happens for one single reason – the wall particles are not in harmony with the particles of our hand. If they were one, the wall would be a natural continuation of our self and would not limit our freedom.

Laws arise as a result of a collision of wills. In a world with no opposing wills, there are no laws, because there is no force commanding the consciousness that it should do this and not otherwise. However, this does not imply that there are no rules in the ideal universe at all. Laws are of two kinds:

- *Internal laws* – the objective logic of the universe on which everything is based. These rules are akin to mathematical theorems and ethical truths, and even God (and above all God) cannot transgress them.

- *External laws* – this kind of laws is formed by a conflict of wills. When two wills come into conflict, the outcome of their conflict is the resultant will, which may not suit both wills, but which they both have to submit to. In this way, laws that inherent in the selfish universe are created.

In our universe, we have a combination of laws of the first and second kind. The aforementioned repulsion of the wall is, on the one hand, the outcome of the separation of the wills. Certainly, the atoms of the wall do not care about our desire to move the wall from its place. On the other hand, it is also the result of the action of true platonic laws, which give stability to our universe. Pushing our hand away, the wall's atoms obey the laws of physics and mathematics, which protect our world from collapsing into chaos. Yes, our hand meets an annoying barrier, but it's better for us at the end of the day. If obstacles of any kind could easily be overcome by a single desire of our will, it is easy to imagine that the imperfect Creation would end up destroying itself literally overnight.

As consciousness enlightens, the laws become "transparent". In the limit, the laws completely disappear. The fully enlightened consciousness (God) does not obey any laws (except for the ideal platonic laws corresponding to the truths of mathematics, aesthetics, and ethics); there is not a drop of "material" in it – it is pure creativity and love.

The simplest representative of the living world is the cell. One of the main tasks of the cell is to dump its entropy into the external world, which is achieved by means of the so-called "metabolism" – the consumption of molecules with lower entropy from the outside world, and the dropping of molecules with higher entropy into the outer world. The resulting difference in entropy is utilized by the cell for the purposes of self-organization and reproduction.

The most important part of the cell is DNA – its genetic program. DNA instructions encode proteins that perform all the work inside the cell. These proteins possess a remarkable property that distinguishes living cells from the inanimate world.

For the purpose of further discussion, let's consider the important notion of a "quantum multiverse" – the ability of a wave function to acquire a set of states simultaneously. Being quantum systems, molecules are able to remain in a multitude of states at the same time. Following the laws of physics, crystal molecules employ a *quantum multiverse* to search for states with *minimal energy*. However, cell proteins, unlike crystals, make use of a quantum multiverse to search for states with *minimal entropy*.

Proteins solve the problem of minimizing entropy by the orders of magnitude more efficiently than crystals. They are designed in such a way that a chemical reaction that is beneficial to the cell will be selected each time against a background of billions of other variants. Being in the quantum multiverse, the protein spreads like a wave, taking the form of trillions of possible configurations simultaneously. As soon as one of these configurations comes into contact with the food molecule, the wave function collapses, and the beneficial configuration of the protein is extracted from the virtual to the physical world, resulting in a chemical reaction that is beneficial for the cell.

Hence, living organisms employ the laws of quantum mechanics as the most effective catalyst for chemical reactions. Proteins do not hope for the opportunity – they explore all possible ways to initiate an advantageous chemical reaction simultaneously.

The use of a quantum multiverse to combat entropy allows living beings to counter the second law of thermodynamics by order of magnitude more successfully than an inanimate world is capable of. The second law of thermodynamics is the law of death. Accordingly, physical systems that apply quantum mechanics for providing effective opposition to the second law can be defined as *living*.

Cognition

Previously, we considered the primary constituents from which consciousness is built – the fundamental blocks of mentality. The fundamental blocks of mentality obey the laws of quantum mechanics, or, more accurately, the laws of quantum mechanics stem from the intrinsic nature of the fundamental blocks of mentality.

Being a quantum system, consciousness is described by the corresponding wave function. Experimental evidence exists which indirectly indicate the quantum nature of our thought process. At a time when the human consciousness does not "float", but is focused on a certain conscious thought, choice, or decision, the neurons of the brain execute the so-called "neural symphonies", working in tact with one another. Synchronous activity of neurons is necessary for the thought process to maintain a stable quantum wave. Let's recall the aforementioned musical analogy: while the musicians are playing in coordination with each other, the symphony of the wave function persists. As long as the wave function of the neurons does not collapse, the mind is immersed in the "world of ideas", extracting all kinds of creativity from there.

Neurons, like the brain as a whole, are just radio receivers that catch the waves of consciousness. By varying our perception (for instance, using music), we alter the tuning to the "radio frequencies" that our brain listens to. The real source of consciousness is located outside the neurons. The root of our insights, emotions, and sensory sensations are the fundamental blocks of mentality.

By analogy with living beings, conscious beings use a quantum multiverse to select states with *minimal entropy*. Only, in this case, we are not talking about thermodynamic entropy, but about *informational entropy*. Unlike living cells, our consciousness seeks optimal solutions not in chemical reactions, but in an enormous set consisting of all sorts of platonic ideas. The neurons of our brain are able to tune into these ideas. It can be assumed that special proteins are present inside the neurons – some sort of "antennas" scanning quantum waves emanating from the fundamental blocks of mentality (the mechanism for amplifying these waves from the Planck scale of the fundamental block of mentality to the neuron scale is considered in the chapter titled "The Universe as a Demiurge Thought"). Making use of a quantum multiverse, these "antennas" listen to an entire set of "frequencies" simultaneously. Among all the perceived frequencies, the neurons select the waves that have the lowest entropy – corresponding with the ideas from ethics, aesthetics, mathematics, or everyday common sense. Furthermore, inside the neuron, the most "interesting" ideas provoke the triggering of synaptic signals from one neuron to another. In this way, additional neurons are activated, and entire groups of neurons are combined to form orchestras.

Any conscious thought is accompanied by a symphony of neurons playing synchronously. Each neuron is tuned to a specific quantum wave (idea) – the synchronous operation of neurons is mandatory for creating harmony within these waves. In this symphony of individual waves, corresponding to particular ideas, new and more complex ideas, thoughts, and insights are born. Thus, using the example of our consciousness, we realize the need for a wave-like, harmonious interaction of quantum particles, without which mental activity is impossible.

Previously, we discussed the way in which living cells utilize a quantum multiverse to search for and implement chemical reactions that are useful to a cell. The same ability to find the optimal variant in the ocean of noise distinguishes conscious beings from the unconscious ones. But, unlike the cell, our soul thrives on creative ideas and meanings. In the ceaseless ocean of informational noise, our consciousness, despite of all the probabilities, is able to snatch out the "juiciest" pieces such as $E = mc^2$ or new musical melodies, similar to the way in which protein cells actualize the most beneficial chemical reaction from trillions of possible alternatives.

Memory and Perception

Hence, the neurons behind the thought process scan the platonic world for ideas in a variety of different frequencies, thereby opening the door to the world of creativity. Before the neurons of memory, there lies an easier task. Neurons of memory do not discover new ideas, but store the already found ones.

Scientific research has established the fact that individual neurons are capable of storing entire concepts. There is a neuron for "green", there is a neuron for "Whitney Houston", there is a neuron for "$E = mc^2$", and so on. It is more than likely that information is duplicated in several neurons, but the point is that a single neuron is capable of storing a complete concept (including the exceedingly complex ones).

But, how can a single neuron of memory be capable of containing the image of one or another personality, emotion, or mathematical idea within itself? It's just one single cell!

Let's consider an example of passive perception – how do we perceive the green color? The particles of light fall on the retina of the eye, and through the cascade of synaptic signals, the information about the photon reaches the neuron, whose "antenna" is pre-tuned to the perception of the green color. The neuron, in its turn, reads the idea of a green color from the world of platonic ideas, and, as a result, we experience a sensation of "greenness". Thus, a single brain cell is capable of storing a whole, arbitrarily complex concept – not in itself, but as a "radio receiver", downloading ideas from their original source – the platonic world of ideas.

The experience of the idea, in this case, occurs inside the fundamental blocks of mentality – we do not require a brain as such to experience this or that idea. The brain is necessary for another purpose – as a tool for synchronizing different ideas with one another (that is, for perceiving different ideas in their relationship with each other) and also as an interface (transfer link) between the fundamental blocks of mentality and our body.

In this regard, let's consider the perception of infants. The immaturity of the infant's brain is reflected by the fact that the world for them looks like a set of fragmented, unconnected platonic ideas. Even the perception of one's own body is deprived of integrity – body movements during the first month of the child's life are chaotic and lack purpose. As the child grows, his brain gradually establishes the connections between various platonic ideas (through the strengthening of synapses linking the corresponding memory neurons). In the process, the brain simultaneously learns to perceive the idea of its own body – in the context of other notions (for instance, the idea of a hand in the context of the idea of food). As the connections between the neurons that are responsible for particular ideas become established, the quantum symphonies of these ideas become possible (and then, we see the child's hand reaching out for the apple). As a result, the world in the child's mind begins to appear as a complete, integrated picture, and his body movements become purposeful.

Personality and Egregores

The human brain consists of about 100 billion neurons. What properties of this ensemble of neurons provide the innate uniqueness to the human *personality*?

Above, we considered an example of how neurons are able to tune themselves to various platonic ideas during the process of thinking and memorizing. The platonic ideas perceived by us can go far beyond the utilitarian, "daily-use" set of concepts and ideas.

One of the most profound platonic ideas that the brain of each individual is tuned to from the moment of birth (or even earlier) is the person's personality as such, i.e. what is referred as the "soul" in religious terms. In the subsequent sections, we agree to call the platonic idea, corresponding to the souls of conscious beings, the "monad" (a term used by Leibniz in a similar context).

Each monad, being a platonic idea, is unique. However, the uniqueness of the monad does not extend to the entire multitude of living human beings. Quite possibly, "copy-paste" is a common occurrence – different people can be tuned to the same monad. Simpler monads are more accessible to perception, and for this reason, they are tuned to by a multitude of "personal" neurons of living people. But, the brighter the personality, the more likely is the possibility that it has "captured" a unique monad.

After tuning in to the monad takes place, a person bears its imprint all his life. Physical extinction and death of a person do not affect the monad, to which he is attuned. At each moment in time, the monad is projected to an ever-changing set of people residing on Earth, representing a kind of plume of its incarnations in our world.

Closely related to the concept of personality is the concept of "egregor". The term *egregor* was used by the famous Russian mystic visionary, Daniil Andreev, in his book titled *The Rose of the World*:

"Egregors are understood as psycho-material formations arising from certain psychic excretions of humanity over large collectives. The egregors are devoid of spiritual monads, but they have a temporarily concentrated volitional charge and the equivalent of consciousness. Every nation has its own egregor, even Luxembourg."

From our point of view, the concept of an egregor is more universal: any harmonious union of conscious elements results in the creation on their basis of an egregor - a new, more complex spiritual entity. The simplest example of an egregor is ourselves – our consciousness is formed by the consciousnesses of a multitude of individual neurons.

Egregor, which is able to attune itself to the platonic idea of a monad, with the help of the latter, acquires an individuality and becomes a "person". Thus, each person is an egregor, but not every egregor is a person.

We can propose the following classification of egregores, based on the increase in their level of complexity:

- Consciousness of elementary particles, united in egregors of atoms/molecules
- Consciousness of molecules, united in egregors of living cells
- Consciousness of neurons (especially important variety of living cells), united in the egregor of human consciousness
- Human consciousness, united in the egregors of individual nations, into the egregor of all mankind and into the egregors of other higher beings (a definition similar to the aforementioned definition provided by Daniil Andreev).

The concept of an egregor clarifies the role of man in the hierarchy of conscious beings. We are by no means the first step on this ladder, and, of course, not the last one. Similarly, just as human consciousness is based on the consciousnesses of the lower entities (neurons), there are egregors of a higher level in relation to us, for which we, the people, play the role of "neurons".

One can draw the following analogy – embodiment in the physical world is similar to programming in a low-level language (i.e. assembler). This is a very laborious task, and numerous basic operations have to be done by oneself, i.e. starting from scratch. While human consciousness serves as a higher-level language for higher beings, with all the amenities inherent to high-level languages, particularly a higher level of abstraction. Therefore, the higher beings prefer to incarnate in our minds, thereby avoiding direct interaction with the "raw" physical world.

The abovementioned classification of egregors is vertical. Egregors can also differ from each other horizontally, i.e. in their spatial coverage:

- The local set of elementary particles forms the egregor of a living cell.
- The aggregate of elementary particles of the Earth forms the egregor of the planet.
- The aggregate of elementary particles of the universe forms the egregor of the entire physical universe.

In this case, the egregors belong to the same level (the level of physical matter), but they have different spatial coverage. The spatial extent of the egregor has a tremendous impact on its ability to engage in a conscious activity (this issue will be discussed in the subsequent two chapters).

PART 2. CONTACT WITH PLATO'S WORLD

Why Are We Alone in the Universe?

In one of the issues of *Scientific American*, a review of the SETI program status was published. It turns out that modern telescopes are several orders of magnitude more efficient in their ability to read signals from space than they were 20 years ago. The conclusion is rather disappointing – if in the following 10 years, any signal from an extraterrestrial civilization is not detected, then, most likely, they simply do not exist in our galaxy.

The Milky Way has 100 billion stars approximately. The estimated number of planets with terrestrial conditions is huge, and is assumed to be, according to minimal estimates, 100 million. Suppose that extraterrestrial intelligence is not detected in the next 10 years. In this case, we are faced with an extremely peculiar mystery: for some reason, among the vast number of Earth-like planets, only Earth hosts intelligent life forms.

Another mystery is the mystery of evolution. Somehow, evolutionary creativity – the creation of exceedingly complex organs right up to the brain – is accompanied by elementary mistakes in the design of the same organs. If we assume that, behind the evolution, stands a highly intelligent, conscious force, then, in this case, we cannot provide an explanation for the primitive solutions and obvious mistakes for which modern engineers would flush crimson. Another question in this regard – why is the process of evolution so painfully slow?

The hypothesis presented in this chapter and the following ones provides a common answer to the aforementioned seemingly entirely different questions. We proceed from the concept of *anātman*, according to which the consciousnesses of all living beings are a manifestation of a single consciousness. This super-consciousness is nothing but "the consciousness" of our universe. Our universe is imperfect. The imperfection of the Universal Consciousness manifests on the various levels of existence, beginning with the material form of existence as such, passing to the ethical problems of the "top of creation" – humanity, and ending with the heat death awaiting the universe itself.

At the level of elementary particles, imperfection manifests in the collapse of the quantum waves of these particles. This collapse can be comprehended as the collision of fundamental wills, in which the wave functions of particles, instead of harmonious interaction and the wave-like exploration of all possible trajectories, collapse and assume a "point" (corpuscular) state.

Just like physical particles, consciousness possesses its own wave function. Obeying the laws of physics, the wave function of consciousness is unstable in spacetime. As in the case of particles, it periodically experiences quantum collapse. While creativity, the processes involving insight and understanding, requires consciousness to remain in a "wave" state – the longer, the better.

The collapse of the consciousness wave function leads to its spatial limitation. What does this mean? The more space is covered by consciousness, the more likely is the onset of quantum collapse. Consequently, to achieve the stability of its wave function, consciousness is compelled to sacrifice its extension in space. Universal Consciousness could, in principle, exist everywhere – but, for a vanishingly small period of time before the onset of another collapse. Or, vice versa – the wave function of Universal Consciousness could exist without a collapse in the cosmic time scales, but at the cost of narrowing down to microscopic spatial coordinates.

A compromise between the spatial and temporal extent of Universal Consciousness is inevitable. And, our planet was chosen to be the location of such a compromise. Earth is unique within the universe, because it is the focus, the localization of the Universe Spirit. It is this unique choice of our planet, and not Darwinism, that explains the emergence and development of living organisms on Earth. It also explains the source of creative forces on the Earth as a whole – starting from the appearance of life and ending with the development of the human mind. Both life and mind are unique in the universe, because in its other, remote parts, its spirit is present to a minimum.

In our experience, we know that the human mind is unable to support two or more lines of consciousness simultaneously. At each moment in time, we concentrate only on one conscious thought. The reason for this is to conserve the "resources" of the consciousness wave function. For the time allotted until the next collapse of the wave function, it is better to ruminate on one thought than to slide over a surface trying to consider several thoughts at the same time. The same argument applies to the "demiurgic spirit", for which the formation of Earth is the primary point of application of its consciousness.

For demiurgic forces, there is no sense in dispersing the resources of the wave function in order to enlighten the materiality of the trillions of planets in the universe. This would irreparably slow down the overall speed of progress, considering that the emergence and evolution of intelligent beings on Earth alone took several billion years. Earth was chosen as a "construction site", on which activities for the purpose of enlightenment are conducted. The creation of additional sites would be counterproductive, since by increasing the spatial coverage of the enlightened consciousness, we end up reducing the time of its stay in the wave state, thereby decreasing its creative potential.

The task at hand is the final enlightenment of the Universal Consciousness. It is possible that a single planet is sufficient to achieve this goal. It can be assumed that when the ultimate goal is accomplished, the resultant effect on the materiality of the universe will be instantaneous and ubiquitous. It is possible that this will be a kind of reversal of the Big Bang. The Earth is the point at which the effort is concentrated, where the partition separating the material world from the spiritual one will be broken. It is for this reason that we are alone in the universe.

Planetary Consciousness

Now, let's move on to the slowness and imperfection of the evolution. Previously, we noted that a greater extent of consciousness in space implies its smaller coverage (stability) in time. Human consciousness expands over the neurons of the brain. This is a rather small spatial dimension, which allows our consciousness to avoid quantum collapse for a long time. During this time, being in a wave state, our consciousness comes in contact with the world of ideas, perceiving all kinds of creative thoughts and insights from there. In this way, we communicate with one another, generate our own ideas, and understand the ideas of others.

The stability of the consciousness embracing the entire planet will be immeasurably smaller than ours. I presume that most of us have watched the movie "Avatar". Our discussion here concerns similar "planetary consciousness". This consciousness, on the one hand, is present in all forms of life on the planet. However, owing to its gigantic size, its temporal stability is vanishingly small – it is subject to continuous quantum collapses.

For the *planetary consciousness*, a few milliseconds of time (the figure is chosen arbitrarily, but it is an exceedingly small time interval) spent without collapse is a luxury that occurs once in hundreds of years, thanks to luck. During these few milliseconds, it executes the so called "evolutionary leaps", succeeding in discovering a more perfect design for living forms and changing the DNA of many living creatures simultaneously. This explains the phenomenon of the origination of new life forms. Then, for centuries or millennia, life is again left to itself, waiting for the next "random window" free of quantum collapses. This idea explains the imperfection of design and the slowness of the evolution:

- Moments when the planetary consciousness does not collapse for a significant period of time are extremely rare and occur once in several centuries. This leads to the slowness of the evolutionary process.

- Even when the planetary consciousness has several milliseconds of time at its disposal, this time is not enough to find the perfect design. Like a chess player under the acute pressure of time, the planetary consciousness chooses the first "acceptable" solution that comes to hand. This explains the imperfection of forms.

The key idea in this regard is that an increase in the spatial extent of consciousness is achieved by sacrificing its temporal extent. Our small brain, and, consequently, our consciousness, are small in power, but we have time at our disposal. Human engineering designs are primitive (by evolution's standards), but they are sound nevertheless, and a more perfect iteration of the product replaces the other in a mere couple of years.

Planetary consciousness, on the other hand, has a planetary scope and phenomenal creative power, but at the cost of an acute shortage of time. When the planetary consciousness gets lucky with time, it is capable of designing a brain in a matter of few milliseconds, the complexity of which still remains beyond the reach of our understanding. But when time is limited – and it is almost always so – the evolution is forced to dwell on intermediate, flawed decisions, the shortcomings of which are obvious even for us.

To summarize, the planetary consciousness is the world champion in chess, who was given 30 seconds for the entire game. Hence, the strange combination of brilliant solutions and elementary mistakes takes places. Human consciousness, on the other hand, is a complete amateur in chess who can ponder about every move for as long as he likes.

Evolution

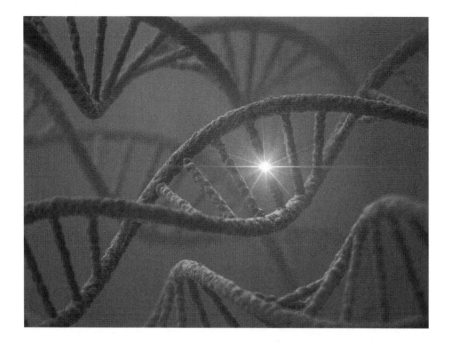

How do evolutionary changes take place in entire species?

A useful genetic mutation that occurred in one individual has practically no chance of surviving. It will inevitably be "washed out" as a result of repeated crossbreeding with individuals who do not have the same mutation. Therefore, the only possible option through which the new beneficial functionality can establish itself in the entire population is the occurrence of massive, simultaneous DNA changes in many individuals belonging to the same species. This implies the existence of a global quantum field – which directly alters the DNA of numerous individuals of the population. Such a global quantum field corresponds to the notion of planetary consciousness that was discussed above.

Now, it's time for a bit of entertaining mathematics. Let's consider the spatial and temporal extension of the human and planetary consciousness:

- The Earth's circumference is 40 million meters; its current age is 5 billion years.
- The circumference of the human head is 0.55 meters; the average life expectancy of a person is 70 years.

How does the temporal extent of consciousness relate to its spatial extent in both cases?

- Relation in the case of the Earth: 5,000,000,000 years/40,000,000 m = 125 years/m
- Relation in the case of a person: 70 years/0.55 m = 127 years/m

– what an extraordinarily interesting coincidence!

Let's consider the smallest living organism as well – the bacterium:

- The size of a typical bacterium is about 1e-6 meters; the lifespan of a typical bacterium in the active state (i.e., the time before its division under favorable conditions) is approximately 1 hour = 1.14e-4 years.
- Ratio in the case of the bacteria: 1.14-4 years/1e-6 m = 114 years/m

– which is practically the same value as in the case of the planet and human!

Considering the completely different scales of the bacterium, human, and planet, the coincidence within one order of magnitude is very surprising. What can such a coincidence indicate? For instance, the consciousness of the many living creatures residing on this planet is made in the image and likeness of the consciousness of the Earth itself.

The dependence considered above is linear – the time of the consciousness existence increases in proportion to its linear dimensions:

$T = kL$

– where T represents the time of the consciousness existence; L represents its linear dimension; and k is a constant whose value is about 120 years/m.

Subsequently, we put forth the following hypothesis:

The duration of the consciousness existence in its "awakened" state (i.e., the state when it is in active contact with the platonic world of ideas) is the same for all beings and does not depend on their size.

Let a represent the temporal stability of consciousness, i.e. the ratio of its stay in the awakened state ($0 \leq a \leq 1$)

Mathematically, the above hypothesis means the following:

$aT = akL = const$

This implies the following:

$a \sim 1/L$

– the temporal stability of consciousness is inversely proportional to its linear dimensions.

Thus, the reason why the planetary consciousness exists many orders of magnitude longer than the consciousness of the bacterium is that, unlike the bacterium, the consciousness of the planet "sleeps" most of the time. *Sleep of consciousness* means that it is in a state of quantum collapse, when its constituent elements are not part of a harmonious quantum wave.

Expressed figuratively, the time of existence assigned to consciousness is like the unfolding of a work of art in time. Every story, every melody has a beginning and an end. And, consciousness is not an exception to this rule. The greater "longevity" of consciousness implies the simple fact that most of the time, this consciousness, instead of "playing" its melody, is just sleeping!

Above, we noted that the temporal stability of consciousness (*a*) is inversely proportional to its linear dimensions. What is the proportionality coefficient in this case?

Let *E* represent the degree of selfishness of consciousness ($0 \leq E \leq \infty$).

Then, the expression for the temporal stability of consciousness can be rewritten as follows:

a = 1/LE

– the egoism of consciousness (*E*), along with its dimensions (*L*), imposes a limitation on its temporal stability (*a*).

Human consciousness, owing to its small size (*L*), is stable in time (*a*). We can create and communicate at will, but our consciousness is limited in terms of its creative power (due to a limited number of basic elements that generate consciousness – neurons).

A significantly more powerful planetary consciousness, owing to its large size (*L*), has negligible temporal stability (*a*). Most of the time, it is in a state of slumber. Within the consciousness, the "neurons" of which are scattered on an area measuring thousands of square kilometers, the intervals of synchronous activity of "neurons" will be very short and, in the overwhelming majority of cases, completely inadequate to have the time to "catch" some conscious thought. Therefore, the creative breakthroughs on the scale of the planet, the so-called "evolutionary leaps", happen very rarely.

At the same time, when by a happy coincidence, a few milliseconds are found at the disposal of the planetary consciousness, it is capable of designing a human brain along with other complex organs in an instant of time and changing the DNA of living beings to implement a new design. Such "windows of luck" last for a few milliseconds – after which the wave function of the planetary consciousness concludes with a quantum collapse. The overwhelming majority of the time, the quantum collapse of the planetary consciousness occurs within nanoseconds – much faster than the time it is able to do anything. Therefore, it seems to us that the evolution has frozen.

From our perspective, the Higher Power, which is responsible for the emergence of life and the further evolution of its forms, is in a state of near-permanent slumber.

But in principle, at any moment, by a lucky coincidence, the planetary consciousness can wake up again for a few moments, having arranged, in front of the eyes of literally single generation, another "Cambrian explosion"...

Waves Vs. Ego (Elementals)

What is the "ego"? An inherent attribute of the ego is the existence of a boundary between the ego and the surrounding world. Through the prism of the ego, we perceive the world around us – as something separate from ourselves.

What is the alternative to the ego? Overcoming the ego entails total rejection of the boundaries. This form of existence might seem speculative. However, our world is filled with creatures devoid of ego, which are inconspicuous and not perceived by us as individuals, but whose existence we feel nevertheless. So-called "spirits of nature" – the spirits of the forests, fields, rivers, mountains – are spread everywhere and have no clear boundaries. We sense their presence, feel their life-force in the air, but we cannot recognize the face behind it – the carrier of the ego.

"Spirits of the places" – elementals – are an example of beings that are free from selfishness, with the wave form of existence. Being omnipresent, and without boundaries, waves are a natural form of the Spirit's existence.

The elementals are nothing but a smaller analog of the planetary consciousness. Not possessing a planetary coverage, i.e. being much smaller in size, the elementals are far less susceptible to quantum collapses, which makes their capacity for conscious activity considerably more stable. This allows to accelerate evolution at the local level – at the cost of a certain decrease in the creativity of the evolutionary solutions. Additionally, the greater stability of the elementals' consciousness makes possible certain kind of communication between people and nature (at an emotionally-sensory, non-verbal level).

From physics, we have the knowledge about wave-particle duality. According to this phenomenon, a quantum particle can possess the properties of a discrete particle as well as a wave. There is a direct correspondence between the notions pertaining to wave-particle duality and the concept of the ego:

- A non-selfish existence possesses wave nature
- While selfish existence manifests in the corpuscular properties

The macroscopic world around us is a continuation of the physics operating in the microworld. The concept of wave-particle duality extends to all conscious beings without exception, including ourselves.

Our ego equates our consciousness with an isolated particle. But, at the same time, consciousness, in its original spiritual nature, belongs to the world of waves. The conflict between the true wave nature of consciousness and the bounds of the ego imposed upon it is constantly felt by us, being the source of many problems. The problem is not the spatial limitation of our brain. At its best moments – in the process of creativity, the experience of love, or the feeling of oneness with nature – the human consciousness is able to go beyond the ego, for some time, becoming a harmonious part of something greater.

There is an essential difference between consciousness in its pure form and the ego. Our real "self" is the monad standing behind us – a platonic idea, a thread of consciousness. Whereas, the ego is a wall erected around our real self. The wall does not add anything to our real self. On the contrary, it only limits its potential and possibilities. The real self has a wave nature. The ego is a kind of breakwater.

As an illustration, let's refer to the analogy with a musical orchestra once again. Each "self" is a musical instrument. Different instruments represent different selves. All selves play in coordination with each other. The orchestra, in its entirety, is representative of God. The ego is when each instrument begins to play its melody as per its desire, out of sync with the rest of the instruments. As a result, a cacophony ensues, which drowns out the individual melody of each self. This results in a selfish, disconnected existence.

The reason behind the emergence of the ego is the linking of consciousness to the set of ethically distorted, deformed platonic ideas that are embedded in the fabric of the universe at the deepest level. Recall the fact that there is no matter as such. Matter is nothing but an egoistic form of consciousness. Everything that is created from matter inevitably inherits the primary egoism that is intrinsic to it.

Therefore, it is not surprising that even after 5 billion years of our planet's existence, a complete deliverance from the ego still seems like an almost impossible feat. To establish the final deliverance from the ego, the physical laws of our world must change, no more and no less.

But, how could the elementals be a happy exception? How could they overcome the selfishness that is inherent in the very foundation of the universe?

The thing is that 5 billion years of life on Earth did not pass without a trace. In the process of formation of the planetary consciousness, it is moving towards its real home – the spiritual world. Our planet has already crossed half this way. Over time, the planetary consciousness will transform the Earth as per the standards of the spiritual world, deploying an ever-increasing set of platonic ideas on it. These ideas are manifested through the beauty of nature, the porfoct forms of living beings, the gentle breezes of wind, the smells of the meadows, the ability to love, etc. From the path that has already been traversed, we can estimate the future direction of the movement. And, there is no doubt that the "gentle breezes" and "smells of the meadows" on this path will increase more and more with time.

The elementals are in the vanguard of this path. Having largely got rid of the ego, possessing a creative wave nature, the elementals have access to the most perfect ideas, many of which cannot be found in any place in the cosmos, except for our common home with the elementals – here on Earth.

Broken Mirror

God is a whole consisting of numerous elements. The whole has a single will, because the wills of its constituent elements are unified (through love). In God, there is a fractal principle – everything is reflected in everything. The whole is displayed in each of the parts, and the parts are displayed in the whole and in one another. As a reflection of the whole, God's constituent elements possess, in the image and likeness of God Himself, free will and consciousness.

For reasons unknown to us, a certain subset of God (conditionally, Lucifer) rejected the principle of "love". It fell away from the whole. Following the fractal nature of creation, Lucifer's constituents repeated his choice. They, like Lucifer, abandoned love as well, putting their will at the head of the corner. Inside these parts, the parts that formed them acted in the exact same manner. And, so on it went. As a result, Lucifer cascaded into many fragments. In this way, during the Big Bang, our universe came into being.

Previously, we have already cited the broken mirror from "The Snow Queen" as a metaphor for the material world. Let us give due to the intuition of the great storyteller – whether Hans Christian Andersen realized this or not – the story of "The Snow Queen" is the story of our world.

Further formation of the universe involves a long way of collecting the mirror fragments and constructing the word – *Eternity* – through them. This is the way to restore the unity of the fallen Lucifer with the whole – God. At the physical level, collecting the mirror fragments is the process that is antithetical to the Big Bang.

Let's note here that "mystical dualism" – the theory concerning the irreconcilable struggle between "good" and "evil" on a global level of existence – is untenable. The defeated, fragmented Lucifer is essentially incapable of fighting with God on an equal footing. The entire "struggle", which indeed does takes place, occurs for the salvation of Lucifer himself, inside himself. If this struggle does not bear successful outcomes, the universe awaits the so-called "thermal death" – a physical state that implies stoppage of time – the final non-existence.

Earth is the only known place in the universe where the "gluing" of Lucifer's fragments occurs at an accelerated pace. This process is known to us as "evolution", and, after the emergence of humanity, as "history".

Evolution has its costs. The consciousness that grows in power, but still has not restored its unity with God, is a potential source of ever-more elaborate forms of evil. In humanity, the potentials pertaining to love and evil are great. They attain their maximum limit in the higher forms of the Universal Consciousness – beings called egregores, demons, and angels.

The consciousness of each individual is a thread of Lucifer's consciousness (the same can be said about the planetary consciousness that stands behind the evolution). Thus, we are all mirror fragments – Kai lives in each one of us. At the same time, the Spirit breathes where it wants; in principle, any spiritual being cannot be entirely isolated from God. This means that in each of us, Gerda lives as well.

Overcoming their fallen nature, the enlightened threads of the Universal Consciousness acquire oneness with God, and through them, thanks to them, Lucifer comes into contact with God, restoring his unity with him. As a result, the desired word, *Eternity*, grows with the next letter.

Previously, we considered the thought process, which is nothing more than the receipt and amplification of the waves of the fundamental blocks of mentality by the neurons of our brain. These microscopic waves (a.k.a. all kinds of platonic ideas) have a size of the same order as the Planck length. They are located on the border of the microcosm, where the very concept of size loses its meaning.

Let us now consider the following illustration of cosmic inflation:

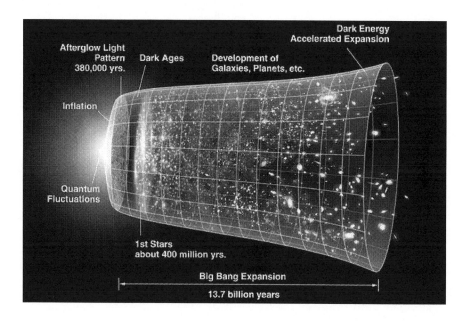

As can be noted from the figure, cosmic inflation increased the microscopic quantum fluctuations of the universe, at the time of its birth, to macroscopic scales, which we now observe in the form of entire galaxies. An analogy with our thought process suggests itself!

In both cases, everything begins with a platonic idea, originating in the microcosm. Moreover, in both cases, the result is amplified to macroscopic scales (neurons of our brain on the one hand and entire galaxies on the other). Therefore, the creation of the universe is analogous to the process of the emergence of thought in our consciousness!

According to scientific data, the random occurrence of an ordered, organized universe like our own has a vanishingly low probability. But, it was not accidental! From the very outset, our universe was a development of the idea of its creator – the demiurge of the universe. Our world is his thought embodied into reality.

Let us now consider three seemingly entirely different theories:

1. The mystical theory of the demiurge who created the universe in his mind
2. The scientific hypothesis that our thought process is based on the amplification of the quantum waves of the fundamental blocks of mentality by our brain neurons
3. The scientific theory of cosmic inflation about the exponential expansion of the universe from microscopic quantum fluctuations

It is quite puzzling that each of these theories can be derived from the other two.

- Hence, the rapid expansion of the universe from microscopic quantum fluctuations (3), combined with the assumption that an analogous amplification of quantum fluctuations is behind our thought process (2), allows us to conclude that the universe is the conscious thought of its Creator (1).

- But, one can also speculate about the theory of cosmic inflation, based on the theories (1) and (2)! If we believe that the universe is the thought of the demiurge (1), while taking into account the fact that our thought process is based on the exponential amplification of the microscopic waves of the fundamental blocks of mentality to the macroscopic scales of the neuron (2), then we can conclude that our universe had to pass through a stage of rapid exponential expansion as well (3) (being the thought realized in the mind of the demiurge!).

- Finally, the seemingly speculative idea of amplifying the waves of the fundamental blocks of mentality by the neurons in the brain (2), against the background of the points (1) and (3) no longer seems to be so speculative. If the phenomenal spatial expansion of quantum fluctuations happened one day at the dawn of our universe, then the same mechanism is capable of explaining the equally grandiose phenomenon of amplification of the waves of the fundamental blocks of mentality in the course of our own thought process.

This is the case when mystical and physical theories go hand in hand, giving each other additional weight.

Modern theory of inflation is far from being complete. In particular, scientists have been discussing specific physical mechanisms that can cause such a rapid expansion of space during the first few moments of the universe's existence. However, if the hypothesis in question is correct, then the Nobel Prize received for explaining the mechanism of cosmic inflation, can also be awarded in another category – as a reward for establishing a physical mechanism that explains the birth of our thoughts. . .

The energy of the universe is zero. And in this regard, there is no mysticism.

Let's ask ourselves the following question: where do the planets take energy from in order to attract mass to themselves? It is known that in order to move the mass to a given distance, it is necessary to expend energy. The more mass we move, the more energy is required. In this case, any planet is capable of attracting all the mass to itself infinitely. But, where does the seemingly infinite energy of the planet's gravitational field, which is required for the infinite attraction of mass, come from?

The answer to this question is paradoxical and simple at the same time. Imagine an object placed at a certain height, which then falls from this height. At the output, we get mechanical deformations (of the Earth and the object itself), as well as the emitted heat. Thus, as a result of the fall of the object, some work was done, which was spent on mechanical deformation and heat generation. The energy to do this work came from somewhere. But, from where?

According to the law of conservation of energy, if there is an increase in energy in one place, it means that it has decreased in some other place. The source of this energy is the gravitational field of the planet. When a falling object expends energy on all possible consequences of its collision with a surface, this energy is subtracted from the gravitational field of the Earth.

It turns out that the reason behind celestial bodies being capable of attracting the infinite amount of new mass to themselves is that the energy of their gravitational field is negative! As a consequence of the attraction of massive object by the celestial body, the energy of its gravitational field increases in absolute value (due to the increase in its mass), while retaining its negative sign. Figuratively speaking, the gravitational fields of the Earth and other celestial bodies take energy on credit. And, this loan is endless for them. The heavenly body will never get tired of attracting a new mass to itself. In this regard, it's like a perpetual motion machine. But, perpetual motion engines, as we know, do not exist. The reason for which mass can be attracted infinitely is that the energy of the gravitational field, while doing positive work, becomes more negative itself.

According to scientific data, the usual positive energy of the universe (in the form of mass, radiation, etc.) is exactly compensated by the negative energy of the gravitational fields. Thus, the universe as a whole has zero energy (and mass).

The question then arises – is it possible for the universe to return to a "zero" state, i.e. to achieve the state when the positive energy of matter and the negative energy of gravity mutually annihilate themselves? This, to a certain extent, will happen with the further expansion of the universe!

According to the laws of physics (the second law of thermodynamics in particular), mass gradually turns into radiation. As a result, the absolute value of the negative gravitational energy (in the form of massive planets and stars) will decrease. As for the positive energy, particles without a rest mass (photons, neutrinos) will begin to dominate in the expanding universe increasingly, and, due to the expansion of space, they will also lose their energy (the photon energy decreases in proportion to the increase in its wavelength).

Thus, cosmology predicts that in the future, a decrease in the negative energy of gravity will be accompanied by a decrease in the positive energy of material particles. This coincidence is not accidental – as these quantities are equal and opposite in sign. In the limit, all celestial bodies will turn into radiation. Radiation, in its turn, as a consequence of the exponential expansion of space, will cool down to zero. There will be no gravity, no mass – nothing. We will return to the state with zero energy.

This state will characterize the maximum entropy, since entropy implies the erasure of differences. The negative energy of gravity is different from the positive energy of matter, and the ultimate disappearance of these last distinguishable features of the universe will accompany the final stoppage of time. Because, in a world in which there are no distinguishable features, nothing can happen.

In the previous chapter, we considered a seemingly fantastic assumption that the process of the origin of thought in our consciousness is analogous to the rapid expansion of the universe in the era of cosmic inflation. This assumption might seem absurd due to the tremendous energies involved in the Big Bang, while our thought process seems to be a completely calm physical process that takes place without any cataclysms. However, as we found out, the boiling activity occurring within the rapidly expanding universe does not, by any means, contradict the fact that the total energy of this universe is zero. This means that the observer external to the universe in principle will not notice any activity – since the zero energy of the system implies that, in a sense, it does not exist.

The same goes for our thought process. Regardless of the nature of the turbulent processes that occur within the world of platonic ideas in the course of their exponential expansion from the Planck scale of the fundamental blocks of mentality to the scale of the neurons – from our point of view – these platonic ideas have zero energy. Thus, the physical security of our neurons is not threatened – the world of platonic ideas, which they work with, has zero energy and, therefore, zero destructive power.

And, finally, the most important aspect – the fact that our universe possesses zero energy (and mass) is a fundamental argument in favor of its non-material, spiritual nature. Mass and energy are attributes of matter. It is obvious that the universe, the total mass of which is zero, is an object belonging to the world of ideas – exactly the same as our own thoughts.

It turns out that being a creator is not so difficult as it seems to be at first glance. To create an entire universe, all that is required is. . . emptiness and a little imagination.

PART 3. REALITY

Holographic Principle

Hence, matter is an emergent phenomenon within the framework of the platonic, spiritual universe. The concept of matter goes hand in hand with the concept of gravity, since gravitational fields are known to be created in the presence of mass. If matter is an emergent concept, does this mean that the gravity that accompanies it is also a derivative of the more fundamental physical laws?

According to the holographic principle, this is precisely the case! The famous physicist, Juan Maldacena, proved (using the example of the special case of four-dimensional space) that a gravitation-free world of *N-1* dimensions, in which particles interact with one another according to the laws of quantum field theory, is equivalent to the gravitational world of *N* dimensions. In other words, the gravitational physical system within a given volume is completely described by the gravity-free processes on the surface that limit this volume.

Extrapolating Maldacena's result to our three-dimensional (3D) world, we can conclude that gravity in the 3D world, just like the 3D world itself, appears emergently from the more fundamental laws of quantum mechanics. These laws, operating on the two-dimensional (2D) surface surrounding our world, represent the real physical foundation of our universe.

The holographic principle found its indirect confirmation in the formula for the black hole entropy, discovered by Stephen Hawking and John Wheeler in the 70s. According to this formula, the entropy (i.e. information) of a black hole is proportional to the area of its surface. Let us imagine that a photon with minimum energy enters the black hole (the minimum photon energy is determined by the condition that its wavelength is equal to the black hole's event horizon diameter). This photon represents a minimum unit of information (1 bit). What happens to a black hole when one bit of information is consumed? According to the formula discovered by Hawking and Wheeler, as a consequence, the area of the black hole's event horizon will increase by one Planck cell! Hence, it can be concluded that the entire volume of information contained in a black hole is stored on the surface of its event horizon, inside cells that are of the size of the Planck length.

Moreover, a black hole is an object with the greatest possible concentration of information. This is due to the fact that any library (with a fixed spatial volume), as more and more books are added to it, will turn into a black hole sooner or later.

From the above, a paradoxical conclusion, consistent with the holographic principle, follows: the maximum amount of information that can be placed in a given volume is proportional not to the volume itself but to the area of the surface surrounding this volume!

Furthermore, the General Relativity Theory (GRT) presents another argument in favor of the holographic principle. According to the GRT, the radial dimension of our space, when passing through the black hole's event horizon, becomes a time dimension inside the black hole. Thus, beyond the event horizon, from the perspective of an external observer, there is absolutely nothing! Since the radial measurement of the external space inside the black hole disappears, the notion of "inside" disappears with it. For us, the entire content of the black hole is located on its surface! However, according to the laws of general relativity, an observer who crossed the event horizon of a black hole will find himself in a three-dimensional world. Thus, a black hole looks like a holographic surface for an external observer and as a three-dimensional world for an observer inside it. Both these perspectives are true – as they are equivalent to each other.

Thus, matter, gravity, and even the usual three-dimensional space, are emergent concepts. In reality, all physical processes happen on a two-dimensional surface that limits our three-dimensional space. The world that is familiar to us appears as a three-dimensional hologram that is projected from the surrounding two-dimensional surface.

What is the "boundary surface" in case of our universe? There is a hypothesis that our world is entirely contained within a black hole. In that case, the "holographic surface" in question would be the event horizon of the black hole. However, certain physical considerations, particularly the observed spatial expansion of the universe, contradict this hypothesis (in a black hole, space must contract).

Another possible candidate for the role of a "holographic surface" is the so-called "cosmological event horizon". It is characterized by the property that the objects located on it are moving away from us at light speed (due to the expansion of the universe). Everything that exists on the other side of the cosmological horizon is in principle inaccessible to our observation, since the particles of light "from there" can never reach us, because the space separating us expands with superluminal speed. The cosmological event horizon, thus, plays the role of an impenetrable barrier separating us from the rest of the universe – similar to the event horizon of the black hole. This might mean (although it is not proved by science yet) that all real physics occur on the surface of the cosmological event horizon, which is rapidly moving away from us.

In any case, regardless of the specific form of the "holographic surface" surrounding our world, the latter, along with the laws of quantum field theory operating on it, is a more fundamental description of our universe. This is a world without gravity and the distortions of space caused by it. This is a world in which one of the three dimensions of space is missing. This is a world that is one step closer to its true spiritual form, in comparison to the surrounding reality that we observe. This world, being two-dimensional, is the literal physical representation of the "mirror" that was discussed in the chapter "Broken Mirror".

Space

From the example of the holographic principle, which essentially abolishes one of the dimensions of space, we observe that the reality familiar to us differs significantly from the real reality (so to speak). If one of the three spatial dimensions can disappear, does not this entail the same ephemerality of the other two?

This question is subtle enough. In general terms, one of the 3D world dimensions can be eliminated because we sacrifice gravity. The resulting equivalent 2D world is already devoid of gravity, so it's impossible to repeat the same holographic "trick" in relation to the 2D world (in order, in its turn, to get a one-dimensional world).

Thus, the remaining two spatial dimensions are the more fundamental property of the world. Nevertheless, it turns out that even these fundamental spatial dimensions possess an emergent nature, stemming from the more basic laws of quantum mechanics.

Let's consider the concept of "quantum entanglement". *Quantum entanglement* is the property of quantum systems in which the quantum states of two objects are dependent on one another. For instance, two quantum-entangled photons located at opposite ends of the universe instantly "feel" each other; measuring the spin of one of the photons will instantly change the spin of another photon. In a certain, or rather even literal, sense, quantum-entangled objects are one whole. If we interpret the quantum system as an information system, then two entangled particles share a common memory address with each other. The information about particles stored in this address describes them as a whole – they are literally one particle.

Employing the holographic principle, what kind of parallels can be established between the equivalent descriptions of the universe in 3D and 2D? In particular, how does the holographic surface encode the third, "missing" spatial dimension?

It turns out that two adjacent cells of 3D space correspond to a pair of quantum-entangled particles from the 2D world! This result reveals the essence of space (which, as we noted above, is an emergent phenomenon).

Space is nothing other than quantum entanglement of particles with one another! To put it differently, space is contained in the interconnections of quantum particles. Moreover, the fabric of our space is smooth due to the fact that the particles forming this fabric are entangled with each other. If the particles were not entangled, it would result in the fragmentation of the universe into completely isolated atoms of spacetime.

The aforementioned points shed light on the reason for which entangled particles instantly "feel" each other, even at great distances. The thing is that, in fact, there is no distance between them at all! Their mutual quantum connection implies their immediate neighborhood in space, even if they are separated by a distance of several light years.

Leonard Susskind (one of the pioneers of the string theory) and above-mentioned Maldacena extended this finding to macroscopic objects. In general relativity, there are the so-called "wormholes" – tunnels in spacetime, directly linking two objects to one another (regardless of the distance separating these objects in the usual space). For instance, according to the GRT, a wormhole can directly connect two black holes that are located far away from each other.

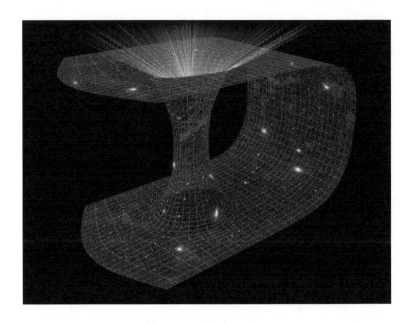

According to the discovery made by Susskind and Maldacena, a wormhole is equivalent to the quantum entanglement of objects located at both ends of the wormhole. This hypothesis is known as *ER = EPR* (ER: Einstein-Rosen bridge – alternative name of a wormhole, EPR: Einstein, Podolsky, Rosen – the names of the researchers who discovered the phenomenon of quantum entanglement).

According to the hypothesis ER = EPR, two black holes that are connected to each other by a wormhole are also connected through quantum entanglement. Thus, the macroscopic phenomenon of general relativity (wormhole) is associated with a phenomenon known from the microscopic world (quantum entanglement).

Conversely, the quantum entanglement of two microscopic particles means that there is a wormhole between them (which, until now, was considered a macroscopic phenomenon of general relativity).

Hence, space is contained within the bonds between the particles. The complete quantum entanglement between the two particles makes them "neighbors" in space. On the other hand, the connection mediated by other particles means their spatial separation. The carrier of space in our universe is a physical vacuum consisting of an infinite number of virtual particles (space cells). Thus, the fabric of the physical space is formed by quantum bonds that exist between virtual particles.

In conclusion, we note that for us, physical space is associated with the freedom of movement. But, in fact, physical space has a dual nature. Space signifies not only freedom of movement but also a *measure of separation*. Standing at a given point on the X axis, we can only have direct contact with our two immediate neighbors – left and right. Then, as far as remote neighbors are concerned, in order to reach them, we still have to overcome the relevant distance.

In the next chapter, we will consider an alternative to physical space – the space of the spiritual world, in which all elements are entangled with one another forming a single interconnected whole. The inhabitants of this world do not need an external, formal space for interaction – they are the space for each other.

Let us ask ourselves the following question: is such a situation possible, when each quantum particle is connected with all the others? Will this result in the disappearance of space and distances as such? If all quantum particles are connected to each other with maximum strength, then the space, while preserving the entire variety of its constituent elements, is compressed literally to a point, since the distances between all particles of space tend to become zero (this situation is antithetical to the aforementioned disintegration of space into completely isolated atoms, the distance between which is equal to eternity).

This question is quite subtle as well. In quantum mechanics, there is a so-called principle of "monogamy of entanglement". As implied by the name of the principle, "polygamy" between quantum particles is strictly forbidden. The "entanglement resource" of a quantum particle is limited – it can be associated in its entirety with only one particle. Simultaneous connection with numerous other particles is possible, but such connections cannot be complete; they will be weakened.

Coming back to the informational interpretation of quantum systems, the amount of "memory" that a quantum particle can share with other particles is limited. A quantum particle can completely share this memory with only one particle (maximum entanglement) or split it into several independent fragments, using these fragments to enter into several partial, weakened connections with other particles.

The monogamy of quantum entanglement is closely related to another property of quantum systems: the prohibition of replicating quantum information (the so-called "no cloning theorem"). This signifies that the memory of a quantum particle cannot be duplicated – it only exists as a single copy. Therefore, if this memory is involved in connection with one particle, it is already inaccessible for forming connections with other particles.

Thus, a complete connection of everything with everything seems impossible, which explains the nature of our space, particularly, the presence of separating distances. The cells of the physical space spend all the "entanglement resource" available to them for establishing links with their nearest neighbors. Following that, it becomes impossible for them to establish additional connections with remote cells in the space. So, here comes a *distance*.

Does this mean that even a pure spiritual world (which, like everything that exists, obeys the laws of quantum mechanics) is doomed to the presence of separating distances?

To answer this question, it is best to turn to the nature of our. . . dreams. Being a product of the creative activity of our consciousness, dreams have the same reality as the universe (which is nothing else but the product of the demiurge of the universe Consciousness). But, unlike the algorithmized universe, with its laws of physics, our dreams are much closer to the true spiritual reality.

What properties does space have in our dreams, and how do these properties correspond with the fundamental properties of quantum systems?

- The ease of movement in space is inherent in our dreams. A certain kind of space is still present, but moving in it does not require any effort and is achieved only by focusing one's attention. We instantly land into any part of the space we want, i.e. we establish any connections with the objects of the spiritual world of our choice and desire. Unlike the rigidly deterministic space of the material universe, in which the "entanglement resource" of the space cell is entirely spent on a narrow circle of its neighbors, in the spiritual space – the connections between the particles are never completely torn apart. By virtue of this phenomenon, one can have 99.99% focus on any of the "possibilities" without breaking the links with the other "alternatives". The choice and change of "possibilities" are carried out with ease – to achieve this simple focus of perception is sufficient. Thus, in the spiritual world, space and distances exist, but they are transient and not static. At each moment in

time, the elements of this space are free to alter their neighbors –
merely by the effort of their thought.

- The fractal nature of the spiritual world plays an important role
  as well. Yes, we cannot enter into a full quantum relationship
  with every element of the "whole", but we do not require it. We
  can treat "the whole" as an independent quantum particle,
  abstracting it from its constituent elements, and thereby form a
  complete quantum bond (at 99.99%) with this whole. For
  instance, in order to find oneself in a dream in one's beloved city,
  we do not need to enter into a full quantum connection with each
  particle of this city. The city appears to us as a single whole; the
  whole is all that interests us – and we establish a complete
  quantum connection with this whole (despite the fact that the
  city comprises of many elements, and we could not possibly form
  a full quantum bond with each of these elements
  simultaneously). Thus, in a pure spiritual world, distances are
  also conditional, because we are not required to communicate
  with individual particles. Instead, we can choose to communicate
  with their aggregates.

Besides dreams, another illustration of spiritual reality is social
networks. Our minds are of a spiritual nature. Hence, it is not
surprising that, as the process of removal of technological barriers
advances, we build communications with each other in the image
and likeness of the spiritual world. The establishment of connections
and communication in social networks is analogous to spiritual
reality:

- Initiating communication does not require effort. In a short
  matter of time, we can easily come into contact with friends from
  different parts of the world. At the same time, in the process of
  communicating with one of the friends, connections with others
  are not broken – they always remain potentially available.

- The monogamy of "quantum entanglement" takes place here as
  well. It is exceedingly difficult to maintain several chat windows

at the same time. At each moment in time, attention is concentrated on only one of them.

- Moreover, just as in the above example with dreams, we can form a direct connection not with individual elements but with the whole. In this case, the "entanglement resource" is not divided into many weakened links with individual elements, but focuses on communicating with their "aggregate". This is nothing more than a *group chat*.

Thus, with the example of dreams and social networks, we can imagine a few of the properties of the spiritual world concerning distances and establishing connections between its elements. The summary of the aforementioned points is as follows:

- Distances in the spiritual world exist, but they can be overcome through the simple focus of attention (perception). At any given time, we can approach any object in this world at any distance we desire (but not all objects at once!).

- Also, perception can focus on objects of different levels – from the primary elements of the spiritual world and their associations to the entire world.

It is logical to consider the physical reality after the spiritual, because it is derived from the latter. Let's ask the following question: what kind of transformation should occur in the spiritual world, so that it appears in the form of everyday physical reality that is familiar to us?

In the spiritual world, the default state involves the ability to communicate directly with everything. The space we are accustomed to does not exist in this world, because the separating distances in it are a mere convention that can be overcome by the simple concentration of attention.

Let's consider the differences between the spiritual and the physical worlds, using the example of a classical quantum experiment with two slits:

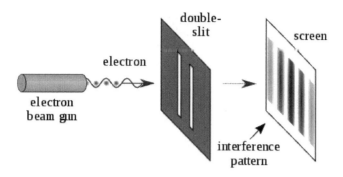

From the presence of an interference pattern on the screen, we can conclude that somehow one single electron flies through two slits at the same time, after which it interferes with itself. The wave function of an electron is as follows:

F = a1 * ELECTRON IN THE LEFT SLIT + a2 * ELECTRON IN THE RIGHT SLIT

– where *a1* and *a2* are complex coefficients.

The same electron, multiplied by certain complex factors, passes through both slits! For us, it looks paradoxical. How can we explain the simultaneous presence of an electron in two different places?

The electron passes through two slits at the same time due to the fact that it is simultaneously entangled with the cells of the space that are located both at the first and the second slit. Even if the number of slits is a million, the electron is able to pass through a million slits at the same time. In fact, the electron does not move anywhere (space is emergent) – the illusion of its movement arises from the consequent entanglement of an electron with the space cells that are in its path. Because the electron travels along all possible trajectories simultaneously, this means that it connects with an almost infinite number of space cells. As we know from the principle of monogamy of entanglement, the entanglement resource of the electron is limited. It follows that the initiation of a huge number of polygamous connections with the space cells is achieved at the cost of a corresponding weakening of each of them.

Simultaneous and the extremely weakened connection of the electron with the multitude of space cells corresponds not to the connection itself but to its "possibility". Thus, a quantum wave can be interpreted as a "wave of possibilities".

Initially, the spiritual world can be perceived as a single quantum system, where everything is connected to everything. This is the reason for the ubiquity of quantum particles in our world – their ability to explore many trajectories simultaneously. An electron "flying" through a million slits at the same time does not multiply into a multitude of virtual copies. There is only a single electron that does not actually fly anywhere. The particle simply establishes relationships with all the space cells that are in its path. Since the electron is entangled with the space cells where the slits are located, it looks as if it is actually "present there".

The connection of everything with everything is a default state; it is a quantum (spiritual) world in its primordial form. Everything is everywhere – not in the sense of a literal stay of the particle in all places at once, but in the sense of a potential "possibility" for it to be everywhere. This makes distances an easily surmountable convention.

Our usual perspective on wonders of quantum mechanics can be reversed in the following manner - miracles of the quantum world, where the particles are present in numerous states at the same time, are not surprising. Surprising is the opposite: what happens to the quantum system, as it, among other things, acquires spatial localization, and classical laws of physics emerge from it at the macro level?

This is an immensely interesting topic, which is at the forefront of scientific inquiry. The reason for which the physical world emerges from the quantum (spiritual) world lies in the phenomenon of the collapse of the quantum waves. As we know from the experiment with two slits, the installation of a detector on the path of an electron (the so-called "measurement") causes the latter to choose one of the trajectories - the first or the second slit. As a result, the interference pattern on the screen disappears. What happens to an electron in the process of "measurement"?

This question is a key question of quantum mechanics. Based on the points explained in the previous chapter, we can conclude that in the process of measurement, the electron focuses its "attention" on one of the "possibilities" available to it. The electron establishes a complete, maximal quantum connection with the space cell chosen by it, at the cost of breaking ties with the other possibilities. Consequently, the electron flies through one particular slit (and the interference pattern on the screen disappears).

But, what exactly forces the electron to focus its attention? We know that the quantum wave of an electron collapses after a detector is installed in its path. At the moment when the electron reaches the detector, while establishing a set of connections with the space cells located in its path, the electron comes in contact with the particles of the detector as well. A certain property of the detector particles distinguishes them from the space cells, making the collapse of the electron wave function an unavoidable occurrence.

This property is the geometric curvature of the bonds of the detector particles!

As is known, space is bent in the presence of energy (or mass). Since the universe as a whole has zero energy (the positive energy of the mass is compensated by the negative energy of the gravitational fields – see the chapter "The Universe that Does Not Exist"), it results in the flat geometry of space at the level of the entire universe. In flat geometry, quantum waves can propagate infinitely, avoiding collapses. However, at the local level, space can be curved by the presence of massive particles. Or, equivalently, mass is nothing but the result of the curvature of the spatial connections! On reaching the massive particles of the detector, a quantum wave of an electron enters the region of curved geometry, which leads to its collapse.

Thus, we are two steps closer to attaining the philosophical understanding of the essence of the quantum collapse:

- First, we found out that quantum collapse is nothing more than the process of "focusing attention" of a quantum particle.

- Second, we found out that the quantum collapse occurs in the region of the curved geometry of space.

What is the reason the curvature of the geometry causes the electron to focus its attention? Here, we can offer a simple analogy – it's sufficient to compare driving on a winding road, which requires a lot of concentration on the driver's part, to a relaxed ride on a straight highway. In the first case, the wave function of the driver's consciousness is constantly collapsing, being forced to constantly extract relevant decisions from the world of ideas, which are related to the situation on the road. In the second case, the driver's consciousness is free to wander in the world of ideas as much as he likes – driving on a straight road practically does not require making any decisions. Certainly, the microscopic consciousness of an electron going through the curved geometry of the detector particles faces a similar dilemma (for more details about the quantum collapse, see the chapter "Collapse of the Wave Function").

Thus, we can arrive at a very important conclusion that answers the question posed in this chapter. The primary difference between the physical world and the spiritual one is that the connections between the particles of the first are twisted, whereas the geometry of the latter is devoid of deformations. The curvature of connections leads to the following consequences:

- The appearance of mass (mass is nothing but a region of space with a curved geometry)

- The collapse of the waves of the quantum particles (the collapse of the quantum waves is nothing more than the rupture of the twisted, "overextended" bonds between particles)

- Emergence of physical space and distances – breaking of the bonds between the particles transforms the spiritual space of "possibilities" (characterized by the connectivity of everything with everything) into a physical space (in which only the adjacent cells of space are connected by a stable connection)

The aforementioned features – the mass, the collapse of quantum waves, separating space – are the primary attributes of the physical world. The physical world is nothing but a curved mirror, in which the "real" – spiritual world – is distorted.

Wave Function Collapse

Measurement is an attempt to learn the truth about an object by comparing this object with our "impression" about it. If the *impression* contradicts the truth about the measured object, the wave function of the object-impression system collapses (the degree of its collapse is determined by the quality of the impression).

The difference between the true state of an object and the impression associated with it is nothing but "curvature". Thus, we can introduce a general, abstract notion of *curvature*:

Curvature is a measure of the contradiction between two platonic ideas.

As a special case, with reference to measurement, the concept of curvature is as follows:

Curvature is a measure of the contradiction between the original idea and the impression of it.

Let's consider the measurement process again using the example of an experiment with two slits. The truth, in this case, is the state of the electron, which passes through two slits at the same time. When we place the detector at one of the slits, we end up asking the "wrong" question, and we get the equally "wrong" answer – the passage of an electron through a single slit.

Thus, measurement is a consequence of our ignorance about the true state of the object. In the process of measurement, we try to relate the measured object to our idea of it. If these two ideas are not consistent with one another, they form curved geometry, and quantum collapse is inevitable. The collapse does not happen solely in one case – when the measured idea and our impression of it do not contradict each other (which means that the geometry formed by them is *flat*).

The evolution of the quantum systems is described by the linear Schrödinger equation, in combination with the spontaneous collapse of the quantum system to one of the possible states as a result of the measurement. The linear evolution of the wave function is conventionally denoted by the letter **U** (**U**nitary evolution), while the nonlinear collapse of the wave function is usually denoted by the letter **R** (quantum wave **R**eduction).

As is known, the Schrödinger equation operates in a linear (flat) physical space. Although space is bent in the presence of mass, but, since gravity is an extremely weak force, the curvature of space caused by the presence of mass is exceedingly small, and these distortions in the laws of quantum mechanics are neglected.

However, it is logical to assume that the linearity of the Schrödinger equation is due to the linear (flat) nature of space! Accordingly, as soon as we take the curvature of the latter into account, the Schrödinger equation inevitably loses its linear nature. In this case, the rejection of the linearity of evolution (**U**) will provide us with the following advantage: we will be able to combine seemingly different processes (**U** and **R**) within the framework of one (nonlinear) equation!

Thus, the linear Schrödinger equation is only an approximation of the true laws of quantum mechanics, in which the curvature of space is not taken into consideration. For such a limitation, it is necessary to pay the price with the introduction of an additional (nonlinear) process – the spontaneous collapse of a quantum wave (**R**). However, as soon as we start taking the curvature of the space into account, in this case, the Schrödinger equation becomes significantly more complicated (due to the loss of its linearity), but the nonlinear collapse **R** will be included in it in a natural way!

From the nonlinearity of the quantum wave evolution, a number of conclusions follow:

- Linear interpretations of quantum mechanics, particularly Everett's many-worlds interpretation, are incomplete, because they do not take the factor of spatial curvature into consideration

- A complete theory of quantum gravity should include a description of the mechanism of quantum collapse (**R**) caused by the curvature of space

We emphasize the fact that the concept of curvature is not exhausted by spatial geometry. Space, as we know, is an emergent phenomenon. Genuine curvature takes place at the level of platonic ideas, and is manifested in the deviation of the ideas from their ideal form or in their wrong relationships with each other.

True platonic ideas never contradict one another. However, distortions of these ideas can be in mutual contradiction. The collapse of the wave function is a forced consequence of such contradictions when two contradictory ideas, while interacting with one another, are compelled to arrive at a "common denominator". This *common denominator* is their state after the wave function collapse.

We also note that the collapse of the wave function is by no means an event that has a negative connotation at all times. Previously (in the chapter "Physical Reality"), we considered an example of driving on a winding road. In this case, the initial idea is our image of the road's geometry (the driver's consciousness generates more and more images with every passing second). Of course, these images are by no means always accurate (it is impossible to predict all the turns in advance), and they come into conflict with the observed idea of the road. As a result, the driver's consciousness experiences a quantum collapse, but this collapse (fortunately for the driver), aligns his image of the road with its true form.

Thus, by virtue of the quantum collapse, we can learn the truth about the object – which is most certainly a positive event. But, even in this case, the collapse is preceded by *curvature* – a measure of our initial ignorance about the true state of the object.

In conclusion, we note that the interpretation of quantum mechanics considered in this chapter belongs to the category of the so-called "objective reduction" (OR) models, which was popularized by the famous English physicist and mathematician, Roger Penrose. According to Penrose, the objective collapse of a quantum system occurs in the presence of spacetime curvature (the latter, in turn, is caused by gravity). We considered the idea forwarded by Penrose as the basis and expanded the concept of curvature from the level of spacetime to the level of abstract platonic ideas. The wave function collapse can occur not only in the region of curved spatial geometry (a special case) but also in the general case of platonic ideas that are in conflict with one another.

Modern physics is far from accepting the wave function collapse as an objective event. For instance, an objective collapse is promptly rejected by Everett's many-worlds interpretation of quantum mechanics. The theory of quantum decoherence interprets the wave function collapse as an apparent phenomenon caused by the interaction of a quantum system (according to the linear evolution **U**) with the external environment. Finally, quantum collapse is not considered as a real phenomenon in the string theory – the leading theory of quantum gravity.

In this chapter, we will consider several additional arguments in favor of the objective collapse theory.

Information Paradox

What happens to information that has fallen into a black hole?

Black holes are not eternal – after a huge period of time has elapsed, each one of them will disappear through the so-called "Hawking radiation" – which is a random, thermal radiation that does not contain any information. However, at the time of its genesis and further growth, a black hole receives a huge amount of information from the external world. According to the generally accepted (based on the linearity of **U**) interpretation of quantum mechanics, quantum information is indestructible in nature. Then, how can the apparent disappearance of information in black holes be explained?

The theory of objective collapse indicates that, ultimately, quantum information can be destroyed. The information is stored in the bonds between the quantum particles. When wave function collapse occurs, these bonds get broken, which implies the destruction of information.

As is known, the gravitational field of a black hole has tremendous power. The spacetime curvature in the neighborhood of a black hole has a maximum value. According to the theory of objective collapse, this means that quantum waves in the vicinity of a black hole will instantaneously collapse. The collapse of quantum waves leads to the breaking down of quantum bonds and the erasure of the information stored in them. Thus, in the vicinity of black holes, information is destroyed owing to the continuous collapse of quantum waves. It is to this hypothesis – the destruction of information in black holes – that modern physics arrived at in connection with aforementioned Hawking radiation (for further reading refer to the so-called "information paradox" discovered by Stephan Hawking).

Destruction of information in black holes solves another problem – violation of causality. The gravitational field of a black hole is capable of bending time into a ring, thereby making the "future" the cause of the "past", which, of course, leads to all sorts of paradoxes. However, in the absence of any information, these paradoxes lose their "sting". The state of the physical system that is devoid of any information is a homogeneous, featureless soup, in which the past is completely indistinguishable from the future.

Flat Geometry of the Universe

Our universe as a whole is a quantum system. To minimize the collapse, the geometry of the universe must be flat. Moreover, considering the enormous mass of the universe, the only way to avoid instantaneous collapse is achieving the ideal flatness of space, which is precisely the observation made by modern science – we live in an ideally flat universe.

Generally accepted interpretations of quantum mechanics do not consider the collapse of the quantum system to be an objective event. Therefore, from their perspective, the geometry of our world in principle could have any form, including the curved one, without any serious consequences. However, if quantum collapse is a real phenomenon, then the curved geometry of space at the level of the universe would lead to major consequences (continuous collapse of the wave function and loss of information as mentioned in the above example of black holes). Therefore, the fact that we live in an ideally flat world is another indirect argument in favor of the objective collapse theory.

ER = EPR

In the chapter "Space", we considered the statement regarding the equivalence of the phenomenon of quantum entanglement (EPR) and wormholes (ER). This hypothesis is quite popular among physicists. However, once "A" is said, one must also be ready to say "B".

As has been established by the GRT, wormholes are extremely unstable objects. A wormhole inevitably collapses when a single photon passes through it! This collapse possesses the objective nature and is caused by the space curvature introduced by the photon. If an objective collapse occurs in the case of wormholes, then, according to the equation ER = EPR, it is just as real phenomenon for the microscopic quantum particles.

To summarize, ideas spread in the human consciousnesses like quantum waves. The sustainability of an idea is determined by the degree to which it, in the final analysis, corresponds to the actual state of affairs. Those interpretations of quantum mechanics that deny the reality of objective collapse are set on a course to experience one. The theory of objective collapse, on the other hand, will spread like a wave, avoiding collapses and being embraced by an ever-increasing number of human minds.

Consciousness vs. Black Holes

At the beginning of the book (in the chapter "Relationship between Matter and Consciousness"), we have considered the difference between matter and consciousness. As we noted earlier, both matter and consciousness consist of one and the same spiritual substance - the fundamental blocks of the mentality. The main difference between matter and consciousness is that consciousness has a wave nature, whereas matter is corpuscular. The wave nature of consciousness allows it to come into contact with the world of platonic ideas, whereas matter, constantly experiencing quantum collapse, is deprived of such an opportunity. For this reason, consciousness is the source of creativity, whereas coarser matter is algorithmized and described by the laws of physics.

Also above (in the chapter "Wave Function Collapse"), we have considered the root cause of quantum collapse: the curvature of platonic ideas – at the fundamental (spiritual) level of existence, and the curvature of spacetime – at the level of the physical universe.

The material presented above (the concepts of *curvature, quantum entanglement,* the *objective collapse* of the wave function, etc.) can be illustrated by the example of the limiting case, namely by comparing the characteristics of the two most polar objects of the universe – consciousness and. . . black holes.

Consciousness and black holes are two opposite extremes of our Universe. Consciousness is spiritual, whereas a black hole is the ultimate concentration of matter. Consciousness, which has a harmonious nature and, as a consequence, a wave form of existence – extracts ideas from the world of ideas, and embodies them in our world (for example, in the living beings – which are nothing but platonic forms embodied in physical matter). At the same time, the maximum curvature of spacetime in the vicinity of black holes leads to a maximally corpuscular form of existence. All objects of our world, encountering a black hole, fall apart into their fundamental components. Recall that the event horizon of the black hole is formed by cells of the Planck size – which can be interpreted as the maximal decay of matter into its constituent fundamental particles – the fundamental blocks of mentality. The complete decay of the quantum system in the vicinity of the black hole into its components is accompanied by a break in the quantum bonds between the particles and the destruction of the information contained in these bonds.

Consciousness, having completed its path, leaves behind new ideas in our world. The black hole on the contrary – destroys the already existing information. In the process of its growth, a black hole absorbs a lot of information contained in matter; at the same time, after the black hole evaporates, all that remains is the Hawking radiation, which contains absolutely no information.

The table below summarizes the key differences between consciousness and the ultimate form of material existence – black holes:

Property	Consciousness	Black hole
Concentration of mass/energy	Minimum	Maximum
Degree of selfishness	Minimum	Maximum
Curvature of spacetime	Minimum	Maximum
Time before the collapse of the wave function	Maximum	Minimum
Quantum entanglement between particles	Maximum, the particles are combined with each other in a harmonious quantum system	Minimum, matter in the vicinity of the black hole breaks up into its fundamental components, of the order of the Planck length

Information	Consciousness constantly retrieves new information from the world of ideas, thereby increasing the amount of information in the physical universe.	Contact with the world of ideas is impossible. Information contained in the absorbed matter is destroyed as a result of the continuing collapse of quantum waves and rapture of quantum bonds, thereby reducing the amount of information in the physical universe.
Spacetime	Consciousness is able to spread in spacetime, harmonizing and integrating its cells into a quantum entangled, integrated whole.	Spacetime is torn into isolated cells of spacetime.
The end result	The merger of a physical system covered by consciousness with its perfect platonic idea, the embodiment of ideas in the physical world.	Thermal (i.e., random) Hawking radiation, which is devoid of any information, the disembodiment of ideas.

PART 4. WHERE DOES TIME END?

Time

According to the theory of relativity, space and time are inextricably linked – in some way, they form a single substance. Therefore, our arguments presented above, on the nature of space, can be extended to time as well, replacing the "cells of space" with the "cells of spacetime". This means that if we have a quantum entanglement between the particles that are separated in space, then the exact same quantum bond should exist in between particles separated in time.

The so-called "delayed choice" experiments conducted during the last 20 years show that this is exactly the case!

Imagine that we are sending out a pair of entangled photons. One of them flies in the direction of the detector located nearby. The second photon flies away much further, say for a distance of several light years, to a remote detector. Since the photons are entangled with one another, the measurement of one of the photons should automatically affect the state of the other. We already know that spatial separation does not preclude photons from instantaneously "feeling" each other (see the chapter "Space").

But, in this experiment, it turns out that the mutual connection of photons is not affected even by their separation in time! Measurements of photons on the first and second (remote) detector correlate with one another – exactly as follows from the phenomenon of quantum entanglement. But, it would seem that the pattern of photons on the first detector cannot depend on the results of measurements at the second detector! By the time the first photon from the pair reaches the first detector, its partner has to fly for a few more years towards the second detector. Theoretically, while the second photon is still flying, we can do anything with the second detector – change its configuration or even remove it. In theory, manipulations with the second detector cannot change the pattern on the first detector – because the first photon from the pair has already landed on its surface, leaving its mark on it.

However, experiments have confirmed that the first photon from the pair interacts with the first detector each time in such a way as if it knows the fate of the second photon in advance (i.e., what will happen to the second photon when it reaches the remote detector). This implies the quantum entanglement of a pair of photons not only in space, but also in time! This is quite consistent with the theory of relativity, which considers the time dimension on the same ground as the dimensions of space (except for the fact that time and space are present in a metric equation with opposite signs).

Thus, from the theory of relativity perspective, time should be regarded as another dimension of space. In this case, our universe, along with its entire history, appears in the form of a static, frozen four-dimensional world.

However, for some reason, our consciousness clearly distinguishes the time coordinate from the spatial coordinates. Time, from our point of view (but not from the point of view of the theory of relativity!), is moving, and we are moving along with it, whereas space is static. This feature of time, distinguishing it from space, will be considered in detail in the chapter "Platonic Ideas".

Clairvoyance and Déjà Vu

The physical mechanism described above – the quantum entanglement of particles in time – makes it possible to elucidate the concept of clairvoyance.

Our consciousness is a quantum field that extends in space and time. Majority of our consciousness is concentrated in the present, which is often (but not always) experienced by us consciously. But, some part of our consciousness spreads in space-time and, like a wave, covers intervals of time in the past as well as in the future. Such travels in time are experienced by us typically at a subconscious level.

Let's assume that in 30 days' time, an event X will happen in my life. This event plays the role of a "remote detector" in the above "delayed choice" experiment. It will be recorded by the part of my consciousness that extends into the future (analog of the second photon in the experiment mentioned above). As a result, the collapse of the consciousness wave function will take place. The part of my consciousness that is located in the present (analog of the first photon in the experiment mentioned above) will change its state accordingly now! Thanks to this occurrence, I can foresee an event X long before it happens in reality.

This idea not only explains the mechanism of clairvoyance but also provides an elegant explanation to the déjà vu riddle. Many people, in certain circumstances, have a strange feeling that "this situation" and the accompanying "emotional background" have already been experienced by them in the past. However, the specific causes behind déjà vu are unknown. Meanwhile, the temporal extent of our consciousness simply suggests itself as a probable reason.

The mechanism of déjà vu is as follows. When extended in time, consciousness observes, in the future, certain situations. Let's take a person's face for example. The collapse of the consciousness wave function takes place (collapse of its "future" part, which also triggers the collapse of the "present" part), and, by virtue of the quantum entanglement between the present and the future, the information extracted from the future is recorded in present memory. All of this happens subconsciously. After a couple of minutes (or maybe an hour, a day, or even a month), the future becomes the present. And, already, in reality, I see a face that seems strangely familiar to me – not only the face but also the whole situation, as they say, "hits the brain", as if it was already experienced sometime earlier!

Where does this sensation come from? This is the result of a memory conflict. The brain, at the time of meeting that person, records its face and the surrounding environment in its memory. But, in the process of recording, the brain discovers that this information is already stored in it – it is already known! Hence, one feels a very specific feeling of déjà vu. We re-experience the event, acutely aware of the fact that we could not have been in this situation before. And, the source of this memory is completely incomprehensible to us.

Clairvoyance differs from déjà vu in the sense that information about the future is remembered consciously, for instance, in prophetic dreams. The moment of re-experience of reality, which you have seen before in a dream, causes a feeling of being surprised and being overwhelmed, similar to déjà vu. But, in this case, the source of the event memory is known (prophetic dream).

Here, I would like to provide a few examples of prophetic dreams from my own experience. Typically, prophetic dreams portend unusual events that go beyond the routine (for example, travel). In my experience, prophetic dreams are characterized by their distinctive clarity and, often, they follow in pairs.

Once, I dreamed that I was inside an industrial structure, something like a factory workshop, and the concrete walls were painted orange. Soon after I saw that dream, my first trip to Washington, D.C., took place. While sightseeing in the city, I tried to find a parking lot for the car closer to the center of the city. It turned out that parking lots in Washington are multistoried structures located underground. Having stopped in one of the parking lots, I found that the first level was full. In search of free space, I drove down, level by level, and the levels differed from each other in color. Finally, at the next level (somewhere fourth in a row), there were vacant parking spots. I got out of the car, looked around, and felt a specific feeling, similar that of a surging wave, in my head. The concrete walls of the level were painted orange – it looked like the industrial structure from my dream...

Here's another example: One time, I dreamed that I was in a theater, sitting in one of the spectator's rows, located at a frightening height. During one of the following days, my wife bought tickets for one of Disney's ice shows (I did not know about her plans and had never been to this theater before). It turned out that our seats were pretty much towering over the row down below, and I sat through the entire show, feeling somewhat tensed, as we had gone there with a four-year-old who "could accidentally fall down".

I have experienced several dozen instances of prophetic dreams in my life. I will conclude with another one. I had dreams about Kansas – the state in which I lived for two years. More specifically, I dreamed of the typical Kansas groves with short trees. After a couple of weeks, I found out that I was due to travel to Austin, Texas. I had never been to Texas before. Soon after my arrival, I went to the nearest park for a jog. And, of course, the trees in Texas were no higher than the ones in Kansas. In front of me, there was a grove of low trees – exactly like the ones in my dream (which, as it turned out, was not about Kansas, but about the upcoming trip to Texas).

Obviously, the ability to foresee the future (with a certain degree of distinctiveness) provides evolutionary advantages to its owners. Therefore this ability should be fairly widespread (with the same frequency as we hear about the evidence of déjà vu experiences) and, in principle, can be confirmed through experiments.

With regard to the example of our smaller counterparts – microscopic quantum particles – similar "delayed choice" experiments were successfully carried out, depicting the principal possibility of such mystical phenomena such as clairvoyance, foreboding, and prophetic dreams.

Let's imagine an astronaut hovering near the event horizon of a black hole. According to the GRT, during a few moments that he spent at the event horizon, he will see the entire history of the universe, scrolled as if in a film accelerated in speed.

Now, let's consider the limiting case. If the astronaut's observation point is directly the surface of the event horizon, then the entire history of our universe will appear in front of him instantaneously. He will see all the events that have ever happened in the universe in an instant! The entire history of our world will appear before him in the form of a static picture, with a time dimension encoded in it, which, however, will be very difficult to discern, because the photons from different times will appear in front of our observer at the same time!

We can say that in this way – in the form of a static picture, with the time encoded inside it – our world looks from the point of view of the "external observer".

At the same time, the universe is nothing but a platonic idea, within which we all live. Accordingly, we can draw a parallel between our world and any other of platonic ideas. Namely, we can conclude that all the platonic ideas are similar "static pictures" containing time within them, just like our universe. The only difference is that, in the case of the universe, we are located inside the platonic idea, whereas in the case of the platonic ideas we perceive, we are the external observers to them.

Many ideas – the idea of green color, circle, different emotions, etc. – are perceived by us in their entirety, and we do not need to unfold them in time in order to comprehend them. However, by analogy with our universe, these ideas have their own internal time dimension.

A good illustration of the "internal time" of ideas is the process of reading books. We read books in a time sequence – page by page, chapter by chapter. At the same time, after the reading has been completed, deeply experienced texts can be felt by us as a holistic, timeless experience. The same goes for music. It is in such a holistic form that the relevant ideas first appear in the mind of their author and then, during their transmission to the mind of others, they are recorded in the form of a time sequence (pages or notes). Thus, in a number of cases, a temporal unfolding of platonic ideas is possible and facilitates their perception.

Let us consider another illustration of internal time from the GRT. It is known that an entire class of solutions of the equations of general relativity contain trajectories that are closed in time. In them, the universe starts from a certain moment in time (t1); then, it evolves in time and space according to the equations of general relativity and. . . returns to the initial point of time t1 (analogous time-closed curves can be obtained in the vicinity of black holes).

Scientists consider these solutions of general relativity to be exotic, which most likely have no analogs in reality. But, in fact, these solutions shed light on the nature of time. They indicate that time can be self-contained and that the future and the past, under certain circumstances, should be perceived as one inseparable whole.

How will an external observer perceive a world that is like a snake biting its tail? He cannot discern the inner evolution of this world, in which the past and the future are indistinguishable. Therefore, the observer will see this world in its complete form, bypassing the process of its unfolding in time; he will perceive it as a holistic platonic idea.

Where does the ability to perceive an process extended in time as an integral whole comes from? In the chapter "Time", we saw that quantum entanglement could connect particles that are separated not only in space but also in time. The integrity of perception arises when the quantum entanglement of the system extends to spacetime in its entirety. All elements of this quantum system are connected to one another. In such a situation, the collapse of the wave function ceases. This state requires the quantum system to achieve the maximum degree of harmony – at this point, the quantum system merges with its ideal platonic image.

The summary of the aforementioned points are as follows:

1. Platonic ideas are all that exists in the world. The world is an ocean of platonic ideas, and our consciousness is like a surfer traveling across the waves of this ocean.

2. When consciousness perceives this or that perfect idea, the internal time of this idea stays out of the equation for us owing to the quantum entanglement (inseparability) of all the elements of this idea in time. We perceive the perfect ideas pertaining to a "circle", the "green color", etc. in their entirety.

3. Existence in time is caused by the presence of "distortions" that break the quantum entanglement of the system. Only because of these distortions, it becomes possible to break the time interval into numerous separate, isolated sectors (moments of time).

4. In the best case, distortion is caused by the natural evolution of creation (the process of cognition), and is a measure of its "ignorance" (or "immaturity"). The ascending hierarchy of

platonic ideas is infinite. Obviously, we cannot be in a quantum bond with the idea that we have not learned yet. In this case, the content of time is the perception and understanding of more and more new ideas.

5. Distortions that violate the unity of spacetime can also be caused by an active denial of truth and by accepting its opposite as truth.

6. The truth that has become a "stumbling block" for our world can possess an ethical nature. We live in the universe, trying to assemble the word *Eternity* from the available pieces (fragments of the once integral, harmonious quantum system). When this word is finally assembled, the ethical offense that led to the creation of our world will be corrected. Spacetime will be harmonized and will become entangled (interconnected) in its entirety. The idea for which this world was created will finally be learned by us. The past and the future will merge into one inseparable whole, and as a result, we will perceive the universe outside of time in its perfect, platonic form.

7. A temporal existence does not end here. The ascending hierarchy of platonic ideas (mathematical, ethical, and aesthetic) is infinite. The discovery of another truth puts forth new questions to us. But, this will happen in another time, in another world. . .

This book is coming to an end. The theoretical questions considered above are the prelude to the two most popular questions: "Who is to blame?" and "What to do?"

Let's start with the first question. The fundamental blocks of creation are the fundamental blocks of mentality – platonic ideas. Every platonic idea is an axiomatic truth, inexpressible in the form of simpler concepts. Any deformation of this idea itself, or the wrong relationship of this idea with other ideas, is a *curvature*. As an example, we can consider the ideal idea of a circle. In this case, any deviation of the circle from its ideal, regular shape will be a curvature.

Of course, the distortion of our world is hardly in the wrong forms of geometric shapes. The deformation that led to the creation of our world has a more complex nature – it is very likely that it is a distortion of a certain ethical truth (or several truths for that matter).

Even if only one truth is deformed, this leads to a chain reaction – all interactions of this truth with the other truths turn out to be distorted as well. For instance, if we had the wrong circle, we would not be able to create the right cylinder (formed by moving the circle along the vertical axis) or the right ball (formed by rotating the circle around the axis).

Thus, a basic set of distorted platonic truths can lead to an entire cascade of problems, because the connections of the original (deformed) truths with all the other truths also become distorted.

Let us list the consequences pertaining to the distortion of platonic ideas (also see the chapter "Physical Reality"):

- Deformation of truths implies the curvature of geometry at the level of platonic ideas. Curved geometry at the level of platonic ideas, in its turn, manifests itself in the curved geometry of spacetime – so here comes a *mass*.

- Curvature of connections between the truths leads to overstrain and periodic rupture in them – the so-called *wave function collapse*.

- Due to the rupture of connections between the quantum particles, spacetime breaks up into divided, isolated cells of spacetime. Thus, the distance along the spatial coordinate arises along with the temporal existence over the time coordinate.

Violation of which ethical idea could lead to all these problems?

One can only speculate. From my point of view, the root cause of such problems is an ethical choice, which is the most difficult for most of us in our own lives. Being a fractal representation of this world's Creator, we after Him, and along with Him, experience the same lesson again and again (and make the same mistakes) until this lesson, sooner or later, is learned.

Here, it is worth mentioning an alternative version of our world – as a kind of ethically neutral "sandbox" – a world created from scratch, containing the potentialities of both good and evil. Why is the version of Lucifer's defection more appealing in comparison to the "sandbox" version?

To answer this question, one can once again turn to the fractal nature of the universe. Conclusions about the origin (and further fate) of the universe can be figured out by considering, as an example, its representatives – us, humanity. The human child is the original, angelic Lucifer. Human children reflect the state of Lucifer before his defection – hence the inherent purity, fun, and spontaneity of childhood. It is clear from this that our world was not created from scratch as the faceless sandbox. At the very beginning, we (i.e. Lucifer) were angelic beings. Youth entails rebellion, defection, but also love. Our subsequent life involves the accelerated scrolling of the fate that awaits Lucifer. Our death reflects the ultimate death of this world.

Everything is reflected in everything. Lucifer owed his original harmony to his openness with the rest of the Creation. The constituent elements of Lucifer were tuned to the rest of the Creation, which was projected on them. The harmony of the whole of the Creation was reflected in the mutual harmony of Lucifer's constituent parts. In other words, for Lucifer, the rest of the Creation played the role of a "compass", which he could use to tune and harmonize his own essence.

One way or another, for one reason or another, there was a defection. Lucifer's connection with the "compasses" was broken. At that moment, Lucifer's constituent elements headed towards an independent, egoistic life – the Big Bang occurred. The essence of Lucifer was literally torn apart from the inside. Spirit became matter.

On this minor note, we arrive at the question "What to do?" In one way or another, the integrity of the initial set of distorted ideas must be restored. The following should lead to the reversal of all other attributes of the physical world:

- Disappearance of mass

- Restoration of the potential connectivity of everything with everything (elimination of distances)

- Merging of all individual moments of time into a harmonious, entangled whole, which will transform our universe into a complete, perfect platonic idea

The quality of good, true ideas is that they do not distort spacetime. Creation, which has a quantum wave nature, naturally evolves in their direction (against this background, distorted ideas lead to spacetime curvature, in the vicinity of which the waves of spirit collapse time and again, making their steady growth impossible).

The Spirit's aspiration for its primordial completeness is unstoppable. The primary driving force of the universe is Love. Enlightenment occurs on a wide front. Not only the initial deformed ideas (which were the root cause of the original defection) but also the broken connection with the compasses, the rest of the Creation, are subject to restoration. Every true idea learned, every act of kindness, every masterpiece of art, every spiritual experience (of nature, love, joy, etc.) contribute to the common cause. We live in a fractal world where concepts such as love and selfishness operate throughout the "ladder" – from the egregors of human communities to the smallest quantum particles. The entire ladder of beings is subject to enlightenment. In the course of this process, we will inevitably observe a change in the physical laws – enlightened matter will increasingly become like consciousness.

The surrounding material world can confound us with its spatial scales. The thought of its global transformation through the efforts of our microscopic bridgehead of spirit – the Earth – might seem to be fantastic.

However, remember that our universe once passed through an era of rapid expansion. At the time of its birth, it was immeasurably "smaller" than the way it is at present (the word "smaller" is not quite correct in this context. At the time of its inception, the universe was not smaller than now – it was more integral – remember that physical space is a *measure of separation*). Also, to this day, our world has a total of zero energy (refer to the chapter "The Universe that Does Not Exist").

Thus, the problem is not the scale of our world and the enormous amount of matter in it. Spatial separation is conditional. The matter, in principle, can return to its ideal, spiritual form. The missing ingredient is the idea, which became a "stumbling block" for Lucifer. This idea is attempting to incarnate in our world, but the geometry of the latter is distorted – the world does not accept it. And, it is quite possible that straightening the universe at the local scale of the Earth will be sufficient to accommodate this idea...

If this happens, at that moment, the physics of the entire world will change. Gerda's tear will find its way to the fragment of ice in Kay's heart. The "Green Door of the Universe" will be flung wide open – here, on our planet. Starting on Earth, the enlightenment of the universe can occur at the same phenomenal speed with which it was created in the era of cosmic inflation. The material universe, in its entirety, will return to its true, spiritual form.

...Gerda and Kay went hand-in-hand towards home; and as they advanced, spring appeared more lovely with its green verdure and its beautiful flowers. Very soon they recognized the large town where they lived, and the tall steeples of the churches, in which the sweet bells were ringing a merry peal as they entered it, and found their way to their grandmother's door. They went upstairs into the little room, where all looked just as it used to do. The old clock was going "tick, tick", and the hands pointed to the time of day, but as they passed through the door into the room they perceived that they were both grown up, and become a man and woman. The roses out on the roof were in full bloom, and peeped in at the window; and there stood the little chairs, on which they had sat when children; and Kay and Gerda seated themselves each on their own chair, and held each other by the hand, while the cold empty grandeur of the Snow Queen's palace vanished from their memories like a painful dream. The grandmother sat in God's bright sunshine, and she read aloud from the Bible, "Except

ye become as little children, ye shall in no wise enter into the kingdom of God." And Kay and Gerda looked into each other's eyes, and all at once understood the words of the old song,

"Roses bloom and cease to be,

But we shall the Christ-child see."

And, they both sat there, grown up, yet children at heart; and it was summer – warm, beautiful summer.

Epilogue

"You may think me superstitious if you will, and foolish; but, indeed, I am more than half convinced that he had in truth, an abnormal gift, and a sense, something – I know not what – that in the guise of wall and door offered him an outlet, a secret and peculiar passage of escape into another and altogether more beautiful world. At any rate, you will say, it betrayed him in the end. But did it betray him? There you touch the inmost mystery of these dreamers, these men of vision and the imagination. We see our world fair and common, the hoarding and the pit. By our daylight standard he walked out of security into darkness, danger and death. But did he see like that?"

— H. G. Wells, The Door in the Wall

Life goes on. . . and passes by
Hard to notice, and so slow
As the years go by and by
I keep on searching for the Door
Yellow leaves lie on the ground
Fields and forests are covered with snow
Time will come – snow will melt down
And the Earth will be green once more
But we'll never be younger again. . .
Blossom of youth is forever gone
Are we immortal? Is there a way?
Is the firmament really firm?
What is waiting for us in the end
When someone will blow the candle out?
Is there a beautiful world out there
The one we have dreams about?
And the blinds will go up and reveal. . .
I know that I've been here before!

Oh my God, I came back, is this real?
I've finally found the Door

Natalia Tsach

Bibliography

Andreev, D. *The Rose of the World*

Conlon, J. *Why String Theory?*

Greene, B. *The Fabric of the Cosmos*

McFadden, J. *Quantum Evolution*

Penrose, R. *The Emperor's New Mind*

Penrose, R. *Shadows of the Mind*

Penrose, R. *The Road to Reality*

Susskind, L. *The Black Hole War*

https://en.wikipedia.org/wiki/Specified_complexity

https://en.wikipedia.org/wiki/ER%3DEPR

Made in the USA
Middletown, DE
02 January 2020